ALSO BY EDWARD KANZE

Notes From New Zealand: A Book of Travel and Natural History

The World of John Burroughs

Wild Life: The Remarkable Lives of Ordinary Animals

Kangaroo Dreaming: An Australian Wildlife Odyssey

"Ed Kanze's Adirondack essays are as lucid as a backcountry pond and as straight and true as an ancient white pine."

-Phil Brown, Editor, *Adirondack Explorer*

"The only thing better and more fun than his writing is Ed, himself. I loved his *Notes From New Zealand* and *Kangaroo Dreaming* and can't imagine how he was able to learn so much and wordsmith his findings and acute observations so beautifully. Whether you are an armchair traveler or a woodsaholic, you will find a lot of beef in these collected works."

-Gary Randorf, author of *The Adirondacks: Wild Island of Hope*

"Using skill, humor, and knowledge born of personal experience, Ed Kanze entices us to join him on a pathway of discovery through the woods and waters of the Adirondack Park."

-Michael G. DiNunzio, author of *Adirondack Wildguide*

"Kanze speaks with several voices: that of the professional naturalist full of accurate information and scientific observations; the skilled writer with a grand sense of humor; the storyteller with a sense of drama; and the adult who has the capacity to view the world through the eyes of a curious child."

-Charlotte Seidenberg, New Orleans *Times-Picayune* writing about Kanze's *Wild Life*.

Over the Mountain and Home Again

JOURNEYS OF AN ADIRONDACK NATURALIST

Edward Kanze

Nicholas K. Burns Publishing
Utica, New York

Nicholas K. Burns Publishing
130 Proctor Boulevard
Utica, New York 13501
www.nkbpublishing.com

First Edition

ISBN 0-9755224-1-8

Cover photo of Moose Mountain © 2006 by Edward Kanze.

Book design by Alyssa Krill/Little Utopia, Inc.

"In Search of Something Lost" first appeared in *Adirondack Life* in the May/June 2004 issue, Vol. 35, no. 3.

"The West Canada Lakes" originally appeared in *Adirondack Life* as "An Adirondack Wilderness: West Canada Lakes," in the September/October 1995 issue, Vol. 26, no. 6.

"Night Voyage" originally appeared in *Adirondack Life* as "Wait Until Dark" in the 2005 Annual Guide, Vol. 36, no. 4.

"Over The Mountain and Home Again" originally appeared in *Adirondack Life* in the 2002 Annual Guide, Vol. 33, no. 4.

"Getting to Know the Neighbors" originally appeared in *Adirondack Life* as "Counting Crows...And Shrews, Slimes and White Pines" in the May/June 2002 issue, Vol. 33, no. 3.

The rest, except for "The Truth about Snow," which has never before been published, have appeared in different form in the *Adirondack Explorer,* the Hersam-Acorn Newspapers, or the Bedford, New York *Record-Review.*

Library of Congress Cataloging-in-Publication Data

Kanze, Edward.
  Over the mountain and home again : journeys of an Adirondack naturalist / Edward Kanze. -- 1st ed.
    p. cm.
  ISBN 0-9755224-1-8 (pbk.)
  1. Natural history--New York (State)--Adirondack Mountains. 2. Kanze, Edward. I. Title.
  QH105.N7K36 2006
  508.747'5--dc22
                        2006017467

For Ned and Tasman

CONTENTS

FOREWORD

Fifteen years have passed since I drove north from Albany, New York with my good friend, author Ed Kanze, towards what would be my first footfalls in the Adirondacks. More interested in chatting, catching up, and eating than I was in the changing landscape that flickered by the car windows, it was not till we arrived at the camp where we would be staying, near Keene Valley, that I sat up, shut up, and took notice.

It is not easy to articulate what makes a mark in the mind, what forges a memory or constitutes a lasting impression, yet when it comes to this book, the author has accomplished all three. Rooted in a landscape that conveys a powerful sense of place, the author sets out not to educate, convert, or convince, at least not entirely. Rather he presents the reader the opportunity to follow a trail of subtle and sublime discovery in a landscape so big, so wild, so wondrous, and so remote in places that few have chosen to share experiences and observations that lead a way through it. Hiking guides abound, but this book represents something new and exciting. Reading *Over the Mountain and Home Again* is like finding a fine wooden chest, the contents of which have been carefully and persuasively placed for the pleasure of anyone who chooses to open the lid, turn a page, reach in, and read on.

I have had the good fortune to spend my life working in great landscapes associated with the power of place and the history of conservation stewardship. Today I live and work in the world's first national park, Yellowstone. As Superintendent I often proclaim to all who will listen the numerous and well deserved superlatives that have been written, spoken, archived, and acted upon about Yellowstone. Yet I feel equal joy and excitement in my heart when presented with this opportunity to do the same for the Adirondacks.

This book will allow readers to discover the power of place that comes to pass through the eye, mind, heart, and spirit of the author, a seventh generation Adirondacker. From macro to micro, from hikes through old growth forest and grand expanses of wilderness to intimate visits with creatures that occupy small and large portions of the landscape, the author leads us over trails, along streams, and up mountains. His tales of nature and adventure will guide you on a powerful, sometimes mysterious journey into the heart of the wild Adirondacks.

Suzanne Lewis
Superintendent, Yellowstone National Park

ACKNOWLEDGMENTS

To the talented and hardworking editors and publishers of *Adirondack Life*, the *Adirondack Explorer*, the Hersam-Acorn Newspapers, and the Bedford, New York *Record-Review*, who helped shape these stories in their original form, then published them, I extend warm thanks. Specifically I wish to credit Betsy Folwell, Galen Crane, Mary Thill, and Tom Hughes at *Adirondack Life*; Dick Beamish, Phil Brown, and Rachel Rice at the *Adirondack Explorer*; Tom Nash, Jack Sanders, and Sally Sanders at Hersam-Acorn; and R.J. Marx and his predecessor Felix Carroll at the *Record-Review*. I'm also in debt to those hardy souls who accompanied me on the strenuous backpacking trips, bushwhacks, and nocturnal canoe voyages described in these pages: Jim Alsina, Debbie Kanze, Fuat Latif, Jeff Main, Sean O'Brien, and Bill Schoch.

At Nicholas K. Burns Publishing, where I'm delighted this book found a home, I'm grateful to the skill and hard work of Nick Burns and his designer Alyssa Krill. Their energy and commitment to the project produced the handsome volume you hold in your hands.

To my wife, Debbie, son, Ned, daughter, Tasman, parents Edward Jr. and Joyce Kanze, sisters Maggie and Nora and their families, grandfather Burdett E. Brownell Sr., and stepgrandmother Florence Luft Brownell, I owe the greatest thanks of all.

Introduction

Two hundred miles and more from Manhattan and visible on the clearest autumn days from Montreal, the Adirondack Mountains form an extraordinary landscape. Rugged peaks loom above deep cool lakes, valleys steepened by Pleistocene glaciers bustle with black bears and beavers, brooks pour over quicksilver waterfalls into creeks, creeks thunder over raging cataracts into rivers, mossy bogs nurture meat-eating plants, and soupy fens sprout exquisite orchids. Forests shaggy with moss, ferns, and a lichen called old man's beard—including the East's most extensive stands of old-growth—mantle slope after rocky slope. For trees, the Adirondacks represent a frontier. Moderately cold-hardy northern hardwoods such as American beech, yellow birch, and sugar maple meet a frigid boreal plant community lorded over by tamarack, spruce, and balsam fir. Stand on a bald summit here, and rare alpine plants gather at your feet. Look down, and you gaze like Zeus or Hera upon a rolling ocean of green.

In search of a spot on the map to settle and build long-term relationships with a place, a community, its wildlife, and each other, my wife, Debbie, and I moved to Saranac Lake, and then Bloomingdale, in the heart of the northern Adirondacks, in 1999. Since tying the knot in a Vermont cow pasture on a windy Leap Day in February 1992, we'd moved often and lived widely. Home places during those eventful years included the Mississippi coast, the wilds of Australia and New Zealand, the Great Smoky Mountains of Tennessee and North Carolina, the Finger Lakes region of New York State, and Acadia National Park on the coast of Maine. "Following our bliss," as Joseph Campbell puts it, we had a grand time, working on and off as National Park rangers and spending the rest of the time writing and traveling.

Steadily, though, a feeling of rootlessness began to gnaw at our spirits. We could rent comfortable apartments, but it didn't change the fact that while a series of roofs kept rain and snow off our heads, we were homeless. Friends, colleagues, and neighbors saw us as transients, and that's how we felt. Envy is an ugly thing, and we began to feel it for people we knew—particularly for those who owned land, loved their home places, and enjoyed happy and supportive relationships with the people next door. We grew ripe for change.

One dazzling blue and orange October, seeking to combine the excitement of wilderness with the purposeful pleasures of community life, to the Adirondack Mountains and their quiet villages we came. For Debbie the setting was largely novel, although together we'd come hiking here on several occasions. For me it felt like coming home. While I would be living year-round in the Adirondacks for the first time, I'd visited every summer during my childhood. We came to visit my mother's father, Burdett Eglin Brownell, whose family had lived in the Adirondack communities of Northville and Hope since about 1800. "Burdy," as his friends called him, was a hero of my childhood, a man who had outgrown most of the recklessness of youth (although until his dying day in 1978, he was always ready to drop everything to go fishing) to become a pillar of a small mountain village long peopled by our ancestors. He was Northville's longest serving mayor. I knew Grampy mainly as a taciturn, wind burned man of the woods who smoked a pipe, spoke softly, waxed thoughtful on every issue that came before him, and liked to take me fishing.

The Adirondack Park is a peculiar place. At nearly 6 million acres, it's larger than the state of Massachusetts and greater in size than Yellowstone, Glacier, Grand Canyon, and Yosemite National Parks combined. But the place is not a park in the same sense. When those exalted national preserves were created, the American Indians and European homesteaders living inside were given the boot. The idea was that if humans inhabited a landscape, it couldn't be wild. In the Adirondacks, the formula was different. The New York State legislature created in 1892 a park boundary, since modified and today known as the Blue Line. The extraordinary thing was that all the people living inside on private inholdings, and timber companies managing their own forest lands, and hotels catering to wilderness-loving tourists, were allowed to remain. Because of that still living history, Debbie and I were able to buy a piece of real estate with an old house on it, a few minutes' drive from two small towns yet surrounded by millions of acres of the wildest land in the East. If it weren't for the bugs and the hard interminable winters, we'd have thought we landed in paradise.

Because I make my living largely as a man of words, I had little choice but to hit the landscape writing. *Adirondack*

Life magazine and the *Adirondack Explorer* welcomed me to their pages, and before long I was a regular contributor in both places. Meanwhile "All Things Natural," the newspaper column I've been writing for the Connecticut-based Hersam-Acorn newspaper chain since 1987, and for the Bedford, New York *Record-Review*, continued to demand an essay from me every week. As columns originating from my new base of operations began to accumulate (to date, I've penned more than 300 in the Adirondacks), the cream floated to the top. The idea for this book was the result.

Over the Mountain and Home Again: Journeys of an Adirondack Naturalist brings together five feature stories that originally appeared in *Adirondack Life*, one essay from the *Adirondack Explorer*, a previously unpublished meditation on snow, and nearly sixty installments of "All Things Natural." I edited, expanded, and rewrote all the material to meld it into a unified narrative. I'm hopeful that Adirondack readers will find pleasure in seeing newspaper material they've never read before, and that my readers in Connecticut and southern New York will find fresh interest in tales that have seen print only in the Deep North. For readers who are new to me and perhaps making their initial acquaintance with the Adirondack Mountains, I extend a special warm hello.

The stories that follow blend science, art, and first-hand observations of Adirondack wildlife and wild places. The text divides itself into thirds. The first section brings together extended journeys deep in the North Woods. Included here is "In Search of Something Lost," a story that won two major prizes: the John Burroughs Association's prestigious annual award for Outstanding Published Natural History Essay in 2004, and a gold medal in environmental writing at the annual conference of the International Regional Magazine Association. It originally appeared in *Adirondack Life*. The book's midsection recounts adventures with that most challenging of housemates, *Peromyscus maniculatus*, known to most people hereabouts as the deer mouse. It also includes a story about a biological survey my family and I have been conducting on the land we share with countless thousands of other living organisms and a previously unpublished essay about deep snowy winters. The final portion provides a portrait of the four dramatic Adirondack seasons as my family and I experience them along the Saranac River near Bloomingdale.

Meander with me if you will, on foot and by canoe, and together we'll explore the life and landscapes of one of the world's great natural places.

Edward Kanze
Bloomingdale, New York
April 2006

I. DEEP IN THE FOREST

In Search
of Something Lost

On a cool, gray July morning that will soon melt into a steamy midday, my friend Bill Schoch and I step out the kitchen door and march into the woods. The blackflies are all but gone, the mosquitoes thin. With few insects to swat, we move quickly on fresh legs, reaching Grass Pond, in the McKenzie Mountain Wilderness Area, in exactly an hour.

Right from the start, I'm feeling like a Don Quixote who has pressed Bill into the precarious shoes of Sancho Panza. The idea for the hike borders on crazy. For three years, in all seasons, I gazed out across the wilderness from our house near Bloomingdale. Time and again, my eyes found greatest interest not on Whiteface Mountain, rising like a ziggurat on the eastern horizon, nor on Moose Mountain, nearer and wearing a landslide like a crooked necktie, but on a low, little-known peak, forested all the way to the top, named Pigeon Roost.

Two-and-a-half miles north and east of Moose, Pigeon Roost bulges 2,769 feet toward the sky. Delving into its history at the public library, I'd confirmed my suspicions about the promontory's name. In the 1800s, and perhaps for centuries before, Pigeon Roost hosted a breeding colony of passenger pigeons.

The passenger pigeon was a native North American bird. It's not to be confused with the carrier pigeon, which is simply a domestic pigeon trained to deliver messages. The passenger pigeon was the most abundant land bird in the world, or so ornithologists believe. Until its numbers collapsed in the middle and late 1800s, the bird migrated North and South through the forests of eastern North America in squadrons so large they challenged the imagination. Early observers such as Alexander Wilson and John James Audubon estimated individual flocks to hold more than a billion birds. Migrating pigeons blackened the sky and broke stout limbs off trees when they landed. Passenger pigeon numbers at the time of the European discovery of America have been estimated at three to five billion. No other species matched that number then, and none does now.

Today, not a single live passenger pigeon remains.

My inspiration for the adventure, or foolishness, was to hike two miles into the woods on an abandoned logging road, then slog more than three miles though woods cluttered with blow-down to reach Pigeon Roost. I resolved to go in late spring or early summer. Call the timing sentimental. I wanted to visit the humble peak when passenger pigeons would have swarmed by the hundreds of thousands.

No one climbs Pigeon Roost today, at least not that I know of. The hill has become obscure. But I felt that someone should go: to honor the birds' absence, to shed a few tears, to remember a species that disappeared forever on September 1, 1914. On that day, "Martha," the last of the passenger pigeons, died in the Cincinnati Zoo.

Bill let himself be persuaded to make the pilgrimage with me, and I'm glad for his company. He's a biologist who understands my motivation. He's skilled with map and compass and will help get us there and home again. He's of my vintage and in a similar state of fitness, so he'll neither wear me out nor slow me down. And most important in a partner for a long, hard bushwhack, Bill possesses an even temper and likes to talk.

When most people in nearby Bloomingdale are home eating breakfast, Bill and I stand at the edge of Grass Pond, watching a great blue heron flap off toward Whiteface Mountain. Behind us lie two miles of brisk but easy walking. Ahead looms our bushwhack: a little more than three miles as the pigeon once flew this territory, almost due east. We'll follow a densely wooded valley that squeezes between Slide Mountain in the north and Moose Mountain to the south. Accurate navigation will be critical. In the deep forest, Pigeon Roost will slip from view. Making things even trickier, our target is one of four promontories—Blue Mountain, Owl's Head, Pigeon Roost, and Mt. Alton—that form a row from north to south. If we deviate even slightly, we'll spend a long, hard day climbing the wrong mountain.

We pick our way across the beaver dam that impounds Grass Pond, then stop to check the map. I've pieced it together by photocopying the corners of four U.S. Geological Survey topographic sheets. Out come compasses, Bill's and mine. Bill also carries a GPS unit, but under the canopy of leaves, its sophisticated scanner can't find a satellite.

As we trudge forward, picking our way over fallen trunks and skirting thickets and boulders, we see little animal life. But we recognize the voices of birds: black-throated blue warbler, red-eyed vireo, Blackburnian warbler, winter wren, swamp sparrow, black-throated green warbler, Nashville warbler, blue-headed vireo, red-breasted nuthatch, American redstart, and hermit thrush. At first, the forest is young, and in one place, it has been freshly burned. Deeper in, we walk reverentially, looking up at the trunks of giants. Bill and I are moved by the thought that these massive, old-growth trees (sugar maple, yellow birch, American beech, eastern hemlock) likely knew the weight of passenger pigeons in their limbs.

Bill wants to hear what I've learned about Adirondack passenger pigeons in general and the Pigeon Roost birds in particular, so through most of the morning, that's what we talk about. Conversation diverts our minds from the grueling work at hand: constant climbing over and around blow-down.

At first, I tell Bill, I found the historical record thin. Adirondack histories tended to leave the passenger pigeon out, despite the fact that probably two out of every five birds in the Adirondacks had been a passenger pigeon when my great-great-great-great-grandparents Daniel and Hannah Brownell settled in the mountains around 1800. The ignorance or avoidance of the subject appalled me. It was as if the tragedy of the pigeon's extinction—no, call it extermination—had been expunged. This in itself would be a tragedy. The passenger pigeon story is a cautionary tale. The thoughtlessness with which our ancestors exhausted a seemingly limitless resource of flesh and feathers brings to mind a twentieth and twenty-first century echo: the civilized world's ravenous consumption of petroleum. Oil and all the products derived from them are marvelous gifts, yet we—I count myself guilty here—burn through the supply like it'll last forever.

Persistence, however, bore fruit. With the help of my friend Andy Keal, a Geographical Information Systems (G.I.S.) expert with the Wildlife Conservation Society, I studied place names on maps. In the Adirondacks Andy and his computer helped me find other probable former nesting sites: Pigeon Hill in Clinton County, Pidgeon [sic] Hill and Big Pidgeon Hill in Essex County, Pigeon Lake in Hamilton County, and Pigeon Mountain in Fulton.

The Mohawk Indians, it seems, called the bird *ourite*. They, like Indians elsewhere in the East, undoubtedly feasted on the pigeons. The Dutch historian Adrian Van der Donck, writing in the seventeenth century in the Hudson Valley, wrote that the "Indians, when they find the breeding places of the pigeons…frequently removed to those places with their wives and children, to the number of two or three hundred in a company, where they live a month or more on young pigeons, which they take, after pushing them from their nests with poles and sticks."

Historical accounts of Adirondack passenger pigeon sightings are few not because the birds were scarce, but, I suspect, for the opposite reason. Commenting on a bird so extravagantly abundant was to state the obvious. Yet a handful of spring, summer, and fall reports come down to us. The botanist Peter Kalm, visiting the mountains in the eighteenth century, saw wild pigeons in the Lake Champlain Narrows and at Crown Point. State Zoologist James DeKay, writing in 1844, called the passenger pigeon "a very prolific species." "The Wild Pigeon, as it is universally called in this country," reported DeKay, "…in certain years…[appeared] in almost incredible numbers, literally darkening the sky and breaking down trees with their weight." In 1863, the naturalist John Burroughs reported "a solitary wild pigeon" at the Upper Works, near

Tahawus. At nearby Lake Sanford, he found the birds "quite numerous." Young Theodore Roosevelt recorded no pigeons while assembling a bird list in 1877 at Paul Smith's. Perhaps the difference between Burroughs's findings in 1863 and Roosevelt's in 1877 affirms something we know from sources outside the region. By the time Roosevelt counted Adirondack birds, passenger pigeon populations were crashing.

Millions of passenger pigeons likely nested in the Adirondack Mountains at any given time. Surely, I thought, at least one of them, as a taxidermic specimen, must "survive." But where? I called the Adirondack Museum in Blue Mountain Lake. Its lone stuffed wild pigeon came from Vermont. The New York State Museum? No luck. The New York State Environmental Science and Forestry School in Syracuse? Same answer. Mike Peterson, one of the Adirondacks' great bird experts, knew of a specimen "collected" (in ornithological parlance this means "shot") by Augustus Paine in Willsboro on October 9, 1891. He said the bird's skin had been transferred to the State Museum in Albany, but I inquired there, and the museum had no record of it. Eventually I found the bird. It had migrated along with the rest of Paine's collection to the American Museum of Natural History in New York. I felt relieved. At least one Adirondack passenger pigeon remains to remind us what can happen when we exploit a natural resource selfishly and government fails to intervene for the public good.

The pigeons of Pigeon Roost leave only a faint trail of paper. John Duquette, writing for the *Adirondack Enterprise* in 1988, told of a William Ryan who, "in the late 1800's," tended dairy cows near Franklin Falls. Ryan apparently managed to drive a wagon near the roost. There, reports Duquette, the "manure" of the pigeons "covered the ground to a depth of 3 or 4 inches." Ryan held his nose, dug the stuff up, hauled it home, and used it as fertilizer. By this time, the pigeon colony had likely been destroyed, but for years afterward, the nutrient-rich effluent would have persisted. (Audubon, traveling in the South, described pigeon guano that "lay several inches deep, covering the whole extent of the roosting place, like a bed of snow.")

According to John Bull's *Birds of New York State*, "the last great pigeon roosting in New York" likely came in 1868, when "millions" of the birds spread their nests over fourteen miles of forest in Alleghany County, near the Pennsylvania border. The Pigeon Roost birds, more remote and perhaps known only to locals, may have persisted longer. John Burroughs saw a last flight of pigeons move up the Hudson Valley in April 1875. Who knows? Maybe they were bound for the place we are seeking.

The bushwhack is taking longer than Bill and I expected it would. Three hours after we left Grass Pond, we are only beginning to climb a slope that, if we've done a good job navigating, will lead to the appropriate summit. We haven't dawdled or stopped to rest for more than a couple of minutes. Even so, our rate of progress through these dense woods measures less than a mile per hour. Passenger pigeons, which had long wings and sleek bodies, were estimated during migration to zoom along at sixty mph.

A little after noon, we come face to face with a wall of rock, garnished with ferns sprouting from crevices and scabbed over in places with lichen. The idea of making a detour holds little appeal, but we don't dare attempt to scale the cliff. Our knees have turned to rubber. Miles from the nearest road, this is no place to break a leg. So we circle to the north and east again, haul our weary carcasses steadily higher, and at last arrive at a view. Through a small opening in the maple and birch leaves, we can see all the way back to Grass Pond.

The moment brings gladness and pain. We see that we've come far, yet it's obvious we're nowhere near the summit. A few hundred feet of climbing probably remain. And there's the matter of all those miles we'll have to retrace on the way home.

When bushwhacking, it's a good idea to set a turn-around time, an hour when, whether you've reached your destination or not, you agree to start homeward. It's easy in the middle of an adventure to say, "Let's go a little farther," and then, "Let's go a little farther still." For every half hour you add to your outbound journey, you have to add another half hour of return. Time is doubled, or tripled because you're growing ever more fatigued. Before you know it, you have too little time for retreat. You rush and twist an ankle, or you struggle out in darkness, or you spend a cold, miserable night under a tree. In the worst case, you die of hypothermia. It happens here, and we know it. At the outset, Bill and I agreed to give up the quest at 1:00 p.m. The time comes and goes, but briefly we persist.

At 1:15, we came to a place where the trees thin, and views open in three directions. In the northeast, we note a rocky prominence, Pigeon Roost's apparent summit. To the south, miles away, we spy Main Street, the Olympic arena, and Mirror Lake in Lake Placid. In the southwest, we look toward the summit of Moose Mountain. Bill's GPS unit still struggles, so I spread the map on the ground like a tablecloth, orient it to true North, and take bearings on the Olympic arena and Moose's summit. The directional lines I sketch intersected on the western flank of Pigeon Roost. Hooray! We've fallen short of the top, but at least we've tramped up the right mountain.

Bill and I dig into our packs for drinks and nibbles. Giving up mosquito-swatting just long enough to take on fuel, we talk about the fact that if this was 1850, we'd likely be seeing, hearing, smelling, and perhaps even lunching on pigeons. Audubon reported that the roar of the birds leaving a roost in the morning and returning at night could be heard for three miles or more. During the day, the female birds sat on eggs or brooded nestlings, at least until the young were ready to clamber through the branches and forage on their own. Mother birds were reported to leave the nest only once a day, while the males commuted to and from feeding grounds often miles away. In the Adirondacks, the pigeons likely gorged on beechnuts, chestnuts, pine seeds, and the fruits of great many woody plants, including elms, maples, alder, birch, pin cherry (formerly known as "pigeon cherry"), black cherry, chokecherry, juneberry, dogwoods (red-osier, gray-stemmed, bunchberry), mountain-ash, sumac, partridgeberry, wintergreen, blueberry, huckleberry, wild strawberry, pokeberry, and more. Nestlings were fed "pigeon milk," regurgitated mostly by the males. The stuff was a blend of ground-up food and parental secretions. Prolactin, the hormone that stimulated the pigeons to produce milk-like nourishment, is the same hormone that provokes my wife, Debbie, to make milk for our baby, Ned.

In trying to imagine what it would have been like to visit an Adirondack roost when pigeons ruled it, we have the benefit of a first-hand account by Albany newspaper editor and travel writer Samuel Hammond. In his 1854 book, *Hills, Lakes, and Forest Streams*, Hammond tells of a visit to a pigeon colony near Tupper Lake. His account is lengthy and detailed, one of the finest descriptions of such a place ever written.

> We were startled, in the gray twilight of the morning, by a distant roaring; not like a waterfall, or far-off thunder, but partaking of both. We heard it several times, at short intervals, and were unable to account for the sound, until, as the light grew more distinct, we saw vast flocks of wild pigeons, winging their way in different directions across the lake....
>
> We paddled down the lake, to a point opposite where [the breeding place] seemed to be, and struck into the woods. We had no difficulty finding it, for the thundering sound of these vast flocks, as they started from their perches, led us on. About half a mile from the lake we came to the outer edge of the roost. Hundreds of thousands of pigeons had flown away that morning, and yet there were hundreds of thousands, and perhaps many millions, old and young, there yet.
>
> It covered acres and acres—I have no idea how many, for I did not go round it.

Wading straight into the colony, Hammond witnessed a scene of biological exuberance unimaginable in the Adirondacks today.

The trees were not of large growth, being mostly of spruce and [stunted] birch, hemlock, and elm, but every one was loaded with nests. In every crotch, on every branch, that would support one, was a nestful of young of all sizes, from the little downy thing just escaped from the shell, to the full-grown one, just ready to fly away. The ground was covered with their offal, and the carcasses of the young in every stage of decay. The great limbs of the trees outside of the brooding place, were broken and hanging down, being unable to sustain the weight of thousands that perched up on them.... Every few minutes, would be heard the roar of a flock of the birds, as they started from among the trees.

Hammond ends his tale in classic fashion. "We struck inland to an island," he writes, "where we breakfasted upon young pigeons, broiled over the coals. They were very fat and tender, and constituted a pleasant change from fish and venison, which, if the truth must be told, were becoming somewhat stale to us."

All the way to Pigeon Roost, Bill and I had joked about the prospect of finding the colony still active—a veritable lost civilization in the jungle, this one populated by birds. Perhaps we'd see what Audubon saw, a wild pigeon "gliding through the woods and close to the observer, it passes like a thought, and on trying to see it again, the eye searches in vain." Of course, we knew this was impossible. Yet some impractical,

Quixotic part of me really did hold out hope of seeing a passenger pigeon. The history of ornithology abounds in birds, long believed extinct, that turn up alive.

My hope, of course, comes to nothing.

If a wild pigeon did materialize, what would it look like? We'd see a bird reminiscent of a mourning dove, with longer wings and a more extravagant tail. The eyes would be colored a dazzling red, the bill black, the plumage vaguely like a dove's but with a gorgeous blue spreading down the head and neck. There would be a metallic iridescence on the nape and shoulder, a smattering of black on the wings, and flanks brick-red or softly purple. Perched, the bird might coo like a domestic pigeon, but with less waver of tone. In flight, it might utter a staccato cry, a sound that reminded Henry Thoreau of the screeching of hawks.

On wobbly knees and plundered feet, Bill and I begin the arduous journey home. All we have left to ponder is the tragic destruction of a magnificent bird, the relentless raiding of the nesting colonies for human food and for the sustenance of hogs, and the heartbreaking convergence of rapacity, prosperity, and technology that sealed the species' doom. The "ifs" in the passenger story are painful to mull. If a strengthening North American economy had not permitted the "trap-shooting" of pigeons to became a popular sport; if railroads had not come along when they did, allowing meat packers in Utica, Plattsburgh, and elsewhere to ship barrels full of iced pigeons to hungry city-dwellers; if weapons that fired breech-loaded cartridges in rapid succession had not proliferated; the passenger pigeon might have survived. But a deck stacked like this couldn't be beaten. The Plattsburgh *Republican* reported, possibly with exaggeration, and possibly not, that 1,800,000 pigeons were shipped to market in 1851 alone.

When the heart of the last Adirondack passenger pigeon pumped its last drop of blood we'll never know. The final report of an extensive flock here came from Henry Felshaw, who witnessed about 300 wild pigeons flying over Constableville, just outside the park, on May 22, 1896. The last known nesting in New York, near Rochester, came in 1904.

Some have argued that the passenger pigeon died out because the forests on which it had depended for sustenance were cut. Biologist A.W. Schorger, author of the definitive book on the species, assembled a mountain of evidence, then concluded this was not the case. "The fact remains," he wrote, "that the supply of beechnuts and acorns was far in excess of the needs of the pigeons throughout the last half-century of their existence."

The truth is ugly. Perhaps that's why it's been kept out of all but a few history books, and why we avoid thinking about it today. The birds nested, as far as we can tell, only in big concentrations. The concentrations were easy to find. People found them. The parent birds were killed, the young were killed, nests were knocked to pieces, eggs were smashed or gathered, and young were snatched for food or spilled into the mouths of hogs or left in the trees to starve. Guns, sticks, stones, clubs, traps, and railroads all played their parts. It was obvious to just about everyone that the supply of birds had no limit. But just about everyone was wrong.

Bill and I make it home before dark. For dinner, there would be none of that old American staple, pigeon potpie. But we do have the pleasure, shortly after peeling off our boots and opening bottles of beer, of looking out the kitchen window and watching a black bear raid a bird feeder. Conservation laws came along too late to save the passenger pigeon, but the bird's horrific loss helped to sound a wake-up call.

Over the Mountain
and Home Again

Every child, woman, and man who has visited the Adirondack Museum in Blue Mountain Lake knows the old, low-tech exhibit that's long been one of my favorites. It shows how early Adirondack tourists found their way to long-gone deep woods hotels via a Rube Goldberg-like series of steamboat rides and railroad runs. In the display, miniature boats and trains shuffle across a relief map, to the accompaniment of a canned narration that's been played so many times it crackles. When I was six, the narrator and his toy trains and boats commanded my attention. More than forty years later, they hold it still.

I believe—one can never be sure about these things—the exhibit sparked an idea that came to me last summer. But before we get to that, a bit of explanation.

My wife, Debbie, and I live within view of Moose Mountain, part of the McKenzie Range that rises immediately north of Saranac Lake and Lake Placid. Although there's no trail up our side of the peak, we'd long aimed to climb it the hard way—straight up through the woods and blow-down.

Motivation didn't come easily. We thought about our sagging muscles, and of the hard work it would take to bushwhack several miles and more than 2,000 feet to the wooded summit. At 3,899 feet, Moose ranks as the Adirondacks' fiftieth highest peak. We found little inspiration, too, in the notion of scrambling all the way to the top, only to retrace our steps on the way home. Circular journeys are more to our liking. Then a brainstorm rumbled straight out of the nineteenth century.

We'd leave our car at home. From our kitchen door, we'd hoof it four miles as the raven flies, and perhaps nearly half again that far on the ground, to stand on Moose's summit. There we'd soak up the view, if any, nurse aches and scratches, and rest before descending a steep but little used trail on the other side. We'd emerge, if we managed to find our way, on the northern shore of Lake Placid. Our destination there was Camp Solitude, a remote bed-and-breakfast that ferries its guests in and out from Lake Placid village.

At Camp Solitude, the adventure would take a civilized turn. We'd eat heartily in the dining room, enjoy a soft bed, and bulk up on hot coffee, scrambled eggs, and bacon at breakfast. Thus refreshed, we'd catch the morning launch into town. From the marina, we'd walk down Main Street to the railroad station, catch the Adirondack Scenic Railway train heading west, and arrive in Saranac Lake for lunch. Now comes the clincher. A hundred feet or so from the restaurant, which overlooks the Saranac River, we'd pick up a canoe, courtesy of Dave Cilley, owner of St. Regis Canoe Outfitters. Eight miles downstream stands our mailbox. We'd paddle there, completing our Victorian-era adventure.

One morning in late summer, off we go. We close the kitchen door at 8:14 a.m., an early start for a couple of late sleepers. A minute's walk from the end of our driveway,

Debbie leads the way down on an old logging road. Before the state acquired the lands hereabouts and protected them as part of the McKenzie Mountain Wilderness Area, the slopes and valleys were clear-cut. The dirt track we follow served as a thoroughfare down which felled giants were hauled to sawmills. We pass a few weather-beaten camps (the Adirondack term for summer house), then cross onto state land. From this point on, the second- and third-growth woods are dark and deep, and we see few signs of humans.

The first hour brings us through a world of beech, birch, and maple. Pine and hemlock elbow in here and there, and a lush growth of knee-high ferns makes the forest floor a salad. Both of us feel fresh and limber. Relishing the cool morning air, we pick our way along the narrow back of an esker created during the last ice age, and when it peters out, we descend to the shore of Grass Pond. As we emerge from the trees, a great blue heron squawks and a belted kingfisher rattles as each flaps toward the far shore. Ahead and above, hidden by an intervening hill, rises Moose Mountain. In plain view to the southwest looms its grander neighbor, Whiteface.

Here we take a deep breath, as one always does before beginning a hard bushwhack, and consult a topographic map. We have three sets of directions for climbing Moose. A neighbor who made the trek years ago said to pick our way across the beaver dam that impounds the waters of Grass Pond. On the far side, he says, we'll find the stream that drains the mountain's slide. (In the Adirondacks, "slide" means a swath of bare rock left behind by a landslide.) The stream will take us to the slide and the slide most of the way to the summit. Simple enough—if it works.

Another veteran of Moose tells us to follow the Grass Pond outlet downstream until we find a major brook feeding it from the south. Follow the tributary upstream, he says, until we come to a fork. Take the fork's right tine to the slide, and the slide to the summit. A third expert points to the most prominent stream on the topo map, one draining Moose's north side and emptying into the Grass Pond outlet. He insists that it will lead us to the slide, and the slide, everyone agrees, offers the easiest route to the summit.

The fact that these directions fail to agree with each other did not surprise us. This is confusing terrain, thick with trees alive and dead, pocked with swamps and marshes, scrambled by beaver ponds, and rife with water courses that twist and turn and plunge in and out of thickets of alder, viburnum, and winterberry. It's hard to spot wildlife. It's hard to see where you're going. We know that while it pays to gather advice, it's more important to carry a map and a compass and know how to use them.

Here's what happens. We tiptoe and wobble across the beaver dam. Finding no sizeable stream on the other side (so much for the first set of directions), we veer westward and pick our way through the woods, following Grass Pond's outlet. Voila! A tributary dribbles in from the south. We trace it upstream, moving under tall beech and maple while tiptoeing around shrubs, saplings, and clumps of wood fern. Summer is well underway. The spring hubbub has ended, and birds and beasts keep silent.

As predicted, the stream forks. We've been told to follow the right branch, but this makes no sense in terms of direction. As we pause to ponder the conundrum, and to question why after heavy rain the stream, which allegedly drains Moose's big slide, has hardly any water in it, we hear a distant sound. It's the roar of a far livelier brook than this one. So we do the sensible thing. We abandon the dribbling stream and bushwhack west to the torrent. It seems to be the watercourse recommended by our third adviser; an impression bolstered a half hour later when the flow veers toward Moose's summit. At last we're on our way.

So we are, but not by the route we thought we'd chosen. The stream does not drain the slide. In hindsight, this is a geographical impossibility. The water pours down a depression in the mountain's flank that common sense says lies to the west of the one scarred by landslide. This is how it can go when you bushwhack through dense woods. You miss one line of movement, but, if your horse sense and orienteering skills are sufficient, you find another that serves the purpose.

Up we go, up, up, up, and, at the risk of sounding repetitious, up. About our three-hour climb to Moose's twin summits, the less said the better. We slog on, huffing, puffing, sweating, hauling ourselves ever higher on steep, rocky slopes filthy with hobblebush. If you've never thrashed your way through hobblebush, you're lucky. The shrub, a type of viburnum, flourishes in the Adirondack woods and has the nasty habit of arching its supple, woody stems down to the ground, where the tips form another set of roots. Natural snares result. They trip even the wary hiker, provoke curses, and, in large doses, bring on despair. The infernal shrub sticks with us nearly to the top, growing thin only after birch and maple gave way to cold-hardy spruce and balsam.

The first of Moose's paired summits we come to, at 2:30 p.m., delivers a magnificent view to the north. For a half hour or more we sit, one by one slipping on layers of clothing we've peeled during the ascent. The sun is blessedly warm, but a breeze spirits away our perspiration and chills us. Binoculars turn up landmarks we know: Route 3 running from Saranac Lake to Bloomingdale, the potato fields of Norman Ridge and Gabriels, Franklin Falls Reservoir, and Grass Pond. Nearly lost in the vista we even spy the roof of our own house, which appears as a speck of red amid a horizon-spanning ocean of green. We can't ask for better hiking weather. The day is clear, cool, and bright.

Eventually we stagger to our feet, find the footpath that will lead us to Lake Placid, and follow it to the mountain's second summit. Here the view makes us gasp. Virtually beneath our feet, so close that it almost seems we could dive into it, spreads the sapphire-blue figure-eight of the lake called Lake Placid (not to be confused with the village of the same name). Its waters are combed by motorboats and divided by two broad, green islands. At the far end lies the village. We pick out familiar brick buildings on Main Street, and at one point, we hear the whistle of an Adirondack Scenic Railway locomotive, pulling from the station.

Past the shops, and far past hills beyond them, rises Mt. Marcy, at 5,344 feet the highest mountain in New York State. Other peaks flank it on both sides. Together the mountains offer a frieze of glacier-sculptured rock and forest, grand and luminous in the warm light of afternoon. We are lucky. I've clawed my way off-trail up other Adirondack mountains, only to find rain, fog, and not a hint of a view at the top. Moose Mountain rewards us generously.

At four o'clock, with the day's hardest work behind us, we move on at a speedier pace. The white blazes of an old Lake

Placid Shore Owner's Association footpath lead steeply down toward Loch Bonnie. Black-capped chickadees flitted around us on the summit, but we find none below. The grandly named Loch, when we reach it, proves nothing more than a small pond, reflecting the forest around it and boggy around the fringes. On we push, losing elevation swiftly. Thoughts of hot water and food begin to shut out our surroundings. We blunder through several trail junctions, following hunches, and to our astonishment emerge on the Camp Solitude lawn. Two friendly dogs bound up to greet us.

Inside the rustic camp, built in 1898, the proprietor, Jay Kelsall, welcomes us. Kelsall's parents operated it in past years as a summer music camp, and still the interior is cluttered with concert playbills, musical instruments, and photographs of smiling students. Every corner seems to hold an upright piano. We are promptly led up a flight of stairs to a cozy pine-paneled bedroom. It's a joy to sit, peel boots off aching feet, undress, and ease hippopotamus-style into a warm, tropical bath.

After dark, dinner is served around a big wooden table. Most of our fellow guests hail from Montreal. Some have come just for dinner, and all want to hear of our journey. We feast on roast turkey, mashed potatoes, gravy, fresh vegetables, salad, and cake warm from the oven. Jean Darrah, the Camp Solitude chef, has done her job well.

Over coffee, we enjoy a concert of original folk songs by Richard Phillips, who accompanies himself on an African thumb-piano. One of the songs strikes me, a lover of literature as well as nature, as unforgettably poignant—an ode to a bag of books abandoned on a city sidewalk.

We sleep like January woodchucks. In the morning, we have time for breakfast and an hour of wry banter with Jay Kelsall on a lakeside porch before it's time to haul gear to the boat. Soon we're off, cruising southward toward the village of Lake Placid with Kelsall at the helm. Green shaggy mountains and handsome rustic camps spring up all around us.

A week at Camp Solitude would have suited us, but it's time to bid Kelsall farewell. We shake his hand, turn an about-face, and walk along leafy side streets to Main Street. There, passing the stolid Hilton Hotel, which stands on the site of a gracious old inn where my mother worked a summer during her college days, we notice tourists eyeing our bulging packs and muddy hiking boots. There's no time to waste. We have a train to catch.

Debbie and I grab a *New York Times* and organic coffees-to-go at a cafe, then bustle past the Palace Theater, Adirondack Steak and Seafood, and the Olympic skating arena. At the railroad station, Debbie secures tickets while I browse the local historical museum that occupies most of the building. The mausoleum of Lake Placid's past is the kind I like best—full of interesting old stuff, presented with a minimum of (but just enough) explanation. In such a place, the mind wanders profitably.

Too soon, the conductor calls "All aboard!" I am a railroad enthusiast, someone who will go out of his way when traveling to ride trains wherever they lead. However, I must admit to having doubts about the satisfaction I'll find in the nine-mile run from Lake Placid to Saranac Lake. I drive the route often. What surprises can it offer? Well, there aren't any, but that's all right. The pleasure of covering familiar ground in a creaky old railroad car is great, and the hobblebush can't touch us.

Windows treat us to a parade of glimpses—of white pine, eastern hemlock, and white cedar, of tamaracks and aspens, of mountains and meadows, of swamps and marshes. People tell us that a man in a bear suit stands waving on the right-hand side of the tracks, but we hurry to the window on that side and find we've missed him. Instead, we note Ray Brook's twin prisons, one that served as housing for athletes during the 1980 Winter Olympic Games, the other a former sanitarium where my great-aunt-Anna cured for tuberculosis during the Great Depression. Soon landmarks in Saranac Lake pop into view: the back side of Pendragon Theater, Pine Hill cemetery, and Bloomingdale Road.

At Saranac Lake station, no one cheers our arrival. We clamber down to terra firma, enjoy a last chat with a volunteer conductor from Binghamton, and scuff down sidewalks to the now-defunct Dockside Grill. There we settle in for cold beer and sandwiches. From our outdoor table, we admire the polished surface of the Saranac River. On the near bank, a rack of canoes belonging to Dave Cilley's St. Regis Canoe Outfitters jazzes up the scene with bright primary colors. Within an hour, we're in one of those sleek boats, slipping downriver.

Until this moment, I have never paddled a canoe other than the kind that Scout troops favor because adolescents are going to demolish them. Cilley, on the other hand, loans us the equivalent of a Rolls Royce, a Mad River model called the Malacite. It has green kevlar skin, wooden ribs, cane seats, and oak gunwales, and it weighs so little that I—hardly a Charles Atlas—can twirl the thing over my head.

Leaving the village, we navigate a set of rapids just lively enough to banish our post-lunch torpor. On we stroke, cruising past landmarks such as Orville Paye's "Gold Mine" miscellany shop and the Saranac Lake sewage treatment plant. The current is gentle, so to get home in time for supper we dip our paddles steadily.

Road noise breaks our reverie at times, but for the most part the voyage yields bliss. We jump in for a swim at one point, cruise through a quiet gorge lined on both sides with the lace-doily foliage of northern white cedars, and disturb the peace of mallards, wood ducks, and muskrats. In marshy stretches, we scan the banks for moose. We never spy one, but we do find the local bus garage, near which moose are frequently sighted. Over a hill to the east lies our house. To get there we have to overshoot it, following big sweeps of the river. In them, the current slows almost to a halt, and oxbow ponds, some stranded, others linked to the main channel, form a maze of navigable water.

Along the way we pass only one other canoe. It contains two friends, Mark and Angela, and we enjoy a chat before waving good-bye. Not long after four o'clock, Moose Pond Road appears and parallels the river on the left. Dead ahead looms Moose Mountain, its north face distinguished by the slide we never found. Much closer, a shiny aluminum enclosure glints atop a wooden post. It's our mailbox.

We've done it! Debbie and I feel a satisfaction in the accomplishment far out of proportion to the mere thirty-two hours and modest amount of energy we've expended. Perhaps the thrill comes from the old-fashioned nature of our adventure, combining as it does various forms of transportation, none of which is the automobile. No doubt, too, we savor the fact that the odyssey begins and ends at the same familiar sight: home.

Night Voyage

All is blackness as I slide a canoe into the Saranac River. My plan, nothing special on the face of it, is to paddle eight or nine miles from Saranac Lake to Bloomingdale. Dozens of canoes make the same voyage every spring, summer, and fall. But as far as I know, no one does it at night.

The morning weather forecast called for rain at day's end. By dinnertime, however, the sky has cleared, and high cirrus clouds, the leading edge of a cold front, promise rain not tonight but tomorrow. My friends Fuat Latif and Scan O'Brian had agreed in advance to join me when conditions seem right. This evening they're perfect. It's June, and a near-full moon will soon breach the horizon. Stars spangle the sky.

Why cruise a beautiful Adirondack river at night, when we'll see little? Call me defensive. Fur bristles on my neck every time an outsider hears where I live and says, "That must be great, but what on earth goes on up there after dark?" I have a stock response. Night life abounds. Being a naturalist and night owl, I buttress my point with tales of bats, bullfrogs, bullheads, flying squirrels, and barred owls. Still, after years of repeating the claim, I'm beginning to wonder if I've been exaggerating. Maybe the Adirondacks really are dead after dark.

Tonight, with the help of Fuat and Sean, both skilled naturalists, I'm heading down river to see who and what is out and about. We'll cruise slowly and silently through the sepulchral world of the Adirondack night. If anything is happening out there, we should get a sense of it.

Fuat is an expert paddler and renowned builder of traditional Adirondack guideboats. Good humored but stern of expression, he takes his rightful place in the stern. Sean is a self-taught bird expert with an encyclopedic knowledge of animal sounds, and he's a bon vivant with a touch of melancholy about him. He leans against a beach chair amidships, sipping a tall black can of Guinness. I'm a naturalist, licensed Adirondack guide, and writer, and I live a mile downstream from Bloomingdale. The property I share with my wife, Debbie, and son, Ned, will be the take-out point. I peer over the bow, straining to hear owls and rails and to spot rocks, logs, and beavers.

The air is still, the river smooth as a sheet of mica. In the East, McKenzie Mountain looms as black as the water.

When we push off, it's 9:30 p.m. The swish of rubber tires rolling northward on Route 3 breaks the silence, then fades along with the car's headlights. The chilly, humid air bites like a dog. I tuck in my shirt, zip a faux-fleece jacket, and regret not bringing hat and gloves.

The first animals we see are bats skimming low over the river. Occasionally one makes straight for my face, then veers off just before impact. I'm not worried. These little marvels cram radar hundreds of times more sensitive than the best the U.S. Air Force employs into flying machines weighing only a few ounces. Bats are far more difficult to identify on the wing than birds. They tend to be colored similar shades of brown, and in low light, it's hard to pick out their field marks, which are subtle. I can't name the species we're seeing. They're medium-sized as bats go and uniformly dark. One thing I am sure of is they're enjoying hearty meals. The night air lays out a smorgasbord of lacewings, caddisflies, moths, mosquitoes, and mayflies.

Minute by minute, our vision improves as the retinas in the backs of our eyes switch from daylight mode to nocturnal. Humans don't possess reflective membrancs behind our retinas, as dogs and cats do, to shine light back on the world and brighten what we strain to see. Yet we adapt. Our pupils dilate, and cone cells responsible for our color vision in bright light surrender the work of sight to rod cells. Rods do their best work in gloom, rendering the world in shades of gray.

My stomach rumbles. Perhaps that's a good thing. Vitamin A in the carrots I ate a few hours ago breaks down in my intestine into a substance called retinal. Retinal finds its way through the bloodstream to the retina, where it combines with a protein, forming a chemical compound called rhodopsin. Rhodopsin is a pigment, and on it the quality of our night vision hangs. When a glimmer of night light falls on the eye, rhodopsin in individual rod cells breaks down, setting in motion a chain reaction that results in the stimulation of nerve fibers. The old saying is true. Eating carrots is good for your eyes, especially in low light. Raw liver offers the same benefit. Old-time mountain men preferred liver, but I stick with carrots.

Good night-vision doesn't happen all at once. Rhodopsin arrives in the retina continually via the bloodstream, but it breaks down in the presence of sunshine. After dark, it begins to accumulate. A half-hour or more of total or near-total darkness must pass before rhodopsin levels rise to the point where our night vision is maximized. Most of us in the civilized world never experience night vision at its best because we're never in the dark that long, except when asleep.

Tonight, our powers of seeing in the dark won't be tested. After only a few minutes in the canoe, the sky pales in the East. Soon a round white moon climbs above McKenzie Mountain. Trees materialize as the leafy river valley develops around us like a Polaroid photograph. If the sky stays clear, the light will soon be bright enough to restore color vision. My jacket, now gray, will turn blue. Something will be gained, but no longer will I see the world as a wolf, fox, or bobcat does, in gothic black-and-white.

This is my first nocturnal voyage down a river, but I'm a compulsive night hiker. The thing I enjoy most about exploring the woods at night is the way my other four senses gain power and attention as sight diminishes. Plunge into the dark, and one becomes acutely aware of sounds, smells, tastes, and textures. That's what happens to us now. We hear with exquisite clarity the sweet, bell-like piping of tiny frogs called spring peepers. Sean whispers "swamp sparrow" as we listen to a lone bird trilling in a marsh to our right. As Fuat steers us under a low bridge connecting Route 3 to Saranac Lake's sewage treatment plant, I note the rich, fetid odor of toilet flushings—not entirely pleasant, but an earthy part of modern life.

Suddenly, as if cued by a maestro, dozens of toads begin to trill. Theirs is a gorgeous performance composed of hundreds of clear, full notes threaded on long strings. These age-old compositions in turn suggest the beaded strings of eggs, some stretching as long as our canoe, that mother toads deposit in ponds, puddles, and backwaters this time of year.

Bats continue darting around us. I wish I could hear them. Their toothy mouths broadcast high-frequency clicks at a steady pace, and the echoes, which may be 2,000 times more faint than the originals, are scooped up by the world's most sensitive ears. Their ears tell the bats about the shape, size, texture, and density of objects they're approaching. Bats see reasonably well, but their vision is nothing beside the tremendous power of their sonar.

Each of the 200 million or so rod cells in my retinas works at collecting every lumen of light out here in the moonlight. There isn't much to go on. Still, I make out the dark water, the outlines of trees and shrubs on the banks, and a foot of mist that floats over the river. The mist makes it impossible to spot obstacles. We'll be jarred by collisions with several floating logs before we're done.

A weird tremolo breaks the silence. We know it's made by a common snipe, a sandpiper relation that prefers inland marshes to seashores. The wavering voice comes again. "It's hard to believe," Sean says, "that the sound is made by the bird's tail." He's right. Wind against feather makes the wail. It's no accident. The bird is making a courtship flight, hoping to stir tender feelings in female snipe on the ground.

Green frogs twang, one here, one there. Fuat observes that we've not heard the loud bass *jug-o-rum* of the bullfrog or the nasal snore of a leopard frog. I suggest the absence may be a matter of timing. I tend to hear leopard frogs a little earlier in the season and bullfrogs somewhat later.

Sean says, "Listen!" He points out a sound I've never heard before, a low staccato *rat-tat-tat*. "A snipe," he says. "This is the bird's ground call." My own knowledge of bird sounds is extensive, but Sean's expertise humbles mine. Not long after this night, he will be recruited by the now-famous Cornell University research team that set off for Arkansas to investigate reports of an ivory-billed woodpecker.

One of the reasons we're cruising downriver tonight is to listen for rails, chicken-like marsh birds that are widely distributed in the Adirondacks but camouflaged, shy, night-active, and rarely seen. It's the final year of the New York State Breeding Bird Atlas Project. We're paddling through a territory Debbie and I have been assigned to survey. Two rail species, the Virginia and the sora, have been found in this neck of the woods in the past. We listen, and listen, and listen some more. Sean's ears in particular miss nothing. Yet the *wak-wak-wak* of the Virginia rail and distinctive whinny of the sora never grace the night.

Suddenly the water ahead erupts like a bomb has gone off. What on earth? A pair of white-tailed deer splash off through the shallows.

Another splash. This one sounds like some joker on the bank has heaved a boulder at us. Yet we're certain there's no joker, and no boulder. A nervous beaver has slapped its tail. The great rodent has alerted its relations and neighbors to possible danger.

A deer snorts somewhere ashore and crashes through bushes toward the highway.

We reach the outlet stream of Moose Pond and decide to paddle a half hour up it. The marshes here, wide and pristine, represent a paradise for rails. Yet we hear only spring peepers, piping by the hundred in groups with silent stretches between them. I joke about the delicate inch-long frogs living in amphibian villages, their peeping posts lined up on sedges and cattails like houses and shops.

A small plane drones overhead, making slow headway toward the west.

The more our ears grow accustomed to the relative silence, the more sounds jump out at us. Fuat points out a faint twittering. Being birdwatchers, we know it for the whistle made by the wings of an American woodcock. Like the snipe, the woodcock is a sandpiper by ancestry. This woodcock has likely been scuttling along the river's spongy bank, probing with its long bill for grubs and worms.

Peepers continue to peep, always in clusters.

Near the bright lights of Saranac Lake's school-bus garage we traverse a stretch of river where moose are occasionally sighted, moving, perhaps, to and from the wetland system that includes the Bloomingdale Bog. Suddenly we're attacked.

One moment all is calm and quiet. The next, angry beasts charge us, shrieking in rage and battering the water. In the bow, where I meet the assault head-on, spray douses the notebook on my lap. We've blundered on Canada geese, likely a mated pair. The birds settle down quickly, and we hear the soft peeps of their goslings.

The river swings east, leaving the road behind it, and courses between low wooded hills. The lazy current zigs and zags through a succession of oxbows, and around every bend lurks a beaver. Explosive tail slaps no longer jar us. We've heard more than thirty, which supports my original contention. Here on the Saranac after dark, things are lively. Beavers look dull and sluggish by day, but they're real party animals. For them a night in late spring is a time for almost frenzied action. Beavers eat, drink, and socialize, and if we could see them better, I suspect we'd observe them playing, fighting, and somehow showing-off for the opposite sex.

At 1:00 a.m., we glide silently past the house of my neighbor Sandy Hayes. His windows are dark, and no doubt Sandy is snug in bed. He doesn't know what he's missing. Bats cavort through the clear cool air over his rooftop, mallards quack at the marshy edge of his lawn, a snipe circles the sky making music with its tail, and a big moon hangs high like a mirrored ball at a discothèque.

Now comes the expedition's finale. The skeleton of a long-dead maple stands on the right bank, silhouetted by the moon. Out of it drops an enormous bird, flapping swiftly and silently away from us, heading downstream. We confer. Sean figures the apparition is a great horned owl. The perch from which the bird flew is too exposed, he says, to appeal to a barred owl, a species that generally keeps to the woods. In the stern, Fuat gets an unsatisfactory look and withholds judgment. In the bow, I probably had the best look of all. My thinking is that the U.F.O. *could* have been an owl, but its great bulk and ponderous wing beats incline me to believe we've scared off a sleeping eagle.

We'll never know. The voyage ends in mystery.

Under a brilliant moon approaching its zenith, my companions and I pull out on a grassy flat and carry the canoe to the house. The cone cells in my retinas are firing now, and I can see the green of the grass and the maroon of the hull's Kevlar.

I drive Fuat and Sean home. At five minutes past two, I'm back again, tired and chilled. I pour a jigger of Scotch, cut it with boiling water, and end the day with a warming nightcap.

Over in Lake Placid, people are still dancing at *Roomers* and *Wise Guys*. I feel certain the revelers would agree with my contention. When night descends on the Adirondacks, things are just beginning to hop.

The West Canada Lakes

Through a vast tract of Adirondack woods, streams, and ponds that may qualify as the wildest place east of the Mississippi, my friend Jim Alsina and I march a rutted trail toward Spruce Lake. Our knees wobble. Our feet throb. Laboring under the first backpacks either of us has carried in years, we have advanced nearly sixteen miles since morning. We woke in a lean-to south of Piseco after being hooted to sleep by barred owls. Now every step pushes us deeper into the West Canada Lakes Wilderness, a 156,735-acre reservoir of wildness that stretches south and west across Hamilton County from Route 30 near Indian Lake until it spills twice over the Herkimer County line.

The terrain has been easy but the trail, like so many in these mountains, has proved rough, an obstacle course of exposed roots and ankle-wrenching hollows. We have one mile to go.

"How are you?" I shout over my shoulder.

"All right." Thud for thud, Jim's footfalls echo mine.

"Is it worth the pain?"

"Ask me later."

Later Jim and I sprawl on the threshold of a lean-to,

nursing sore shoulders, aching legs, and blisters. Clear blue water spreads before us. Beyond in the west rise low mountains, wooded in balsam fir, red spruce, American beech, and four kinds of maple—sugar, red, striped, and mountain. Just out of sight, a loon calls. Its demented laughter brings smiles to our grim faces. Jim finally answers my question. "This is heaven."

Heaven remains heavenly as the lake sinks into darkness and several thousand stars blink on one by one. For an hour, we do nothing but sit on rocks at the water's edge, enjoying the contrast between the warmth of the stone and the cool night air while marveling at the immensity of the star-dusted sky. Then serenity turns to horror. Two military jets appear over the western hills and race toward us. Flying just above the balsam spires, they scream and thunder directly overhead and lash us with their lights. Silence returns, but the spell is beyond mending.

Look at the West Canada Lakes Wilderness on a map and you see a shape like that of a headless, narrow-waisted man or woman hurling a javelin. Spruce Lake lies at the belly. Now, fueled by powdered orange juice and lumpy instant oatmeal, we hurry toward the heart, toward a cluster of clear, cold lakes known as the West Canadas.

I scowl and curse blisters that are fast becoming open wounds. Jim complains of muscle cramps. Mile after merciless mile, hardly glancing at glorious maples painted red and orange by autumn, we advance. We have failed to heed a cardinal rule of backpacking. If out of shape at the beginning of a journey, start with a few days of easy walking so muscles can strengthen and feet grow tough with calluses. Instead, with cheerless determination, we pursue our aim to hike the Northville-Lake Placid Trail from Benson to Averyville in ten days.

At midday, we break loose of dark forest and find ourselves on the sunny shore of a lake. This is 250-acre West Lake, the biggest of the West Canadas. The hermit known as French Louie lived here from about 1875 until 1918. Born Louis Seymour, he was renowned for his prowess as a trapper and woodsman as well as for a love of solitude and whiskey. My mother's father, Burdett Brownell of Northville, born in 1904, met Louie when the hermit was old and grizzled. Having heard my grandfather speak of Louie, I have long wanted to visit the trapper's haunts. Here I am, yet our arbitrary schedule allows for no lingering. With only a glance at a long, striped garter snake we found in the ruin of Louie's fireplace, we turn our backs on the indigo-blue lake and stagger onward. I wonder, during a moment when my mind drifts away from blisters, if the serpent is a great-grand-snake of the garters Louie put in his vegetable garden to eat pestiferous insects.

Late in the afternoon, after hours of tromping through dense and lonely forest, we reach the Cedar Lakes, a collection of ponds and swamps that sprawl north and east of the West Canadas. We collapse on the decking of a footbridge. It's time for a talk.

Jim and I concede we're pushing too hard. And we agree that we've underestimated the appeal of the West Canada Lakes Wilderness. Among designated Adirondack wilderness lands, this place is second in size only to the High Peaks. Yet it receives only a fraction of the visitors. We have seen no other hikers in four days, save for two brawny Minnesotans we met at the Piseco post office. (The Northville-Placid trail leaves the woods at the tiny village, passes briefly through civilization, and plunges back into forest.) Access is limited to a few trunk trails, black bear and beaver abound, and the woods—logged earlier than most in the Adirondacks and well healed now—are thick and largely trackless. Jim and I are won over by some of the finest hills, valleys, forests, and lakes either of us has ever seen.

In the golden sunshine on the footbridge, we reach a momentous decision. To hell with our plan! We're staying here. Feeling as joyously free as prisoners released from long captivity, we shake off packs, peel off boots, and slow down and smell the balsam.

In an instant the entire character of our trek through the West Canada Lakes changes. It's like the moment in *The Wizard of Oz* when the film shifts from black-and-white to color. We look around and find ourselves in a wonderland, immersed in leafy beauty, the path ahead no longer a trail of tears but a shining, enticing yellow brick road.

We set up camp in a lean-to beside the foundation of a ranger's cabin destroyed by the New York State Department of Environmental Conservation after the state declared the tract wilderness. On the lean-to's walls, we find graffiti, including sentimental farewells ("J.R. was here") and political commentary ("The Sierra Club sucks"). The afternoon sun, soft and tangerine-colored, bathes us in an Elysian glow matched by our rising spirits. We rest. We cook. We savor our food. We laugh. We watch loons and mergansers cruise the lake, listen to the cry of an osprey that circles in the sky, and rejoice in the fact that the world, for all its faults, still harbors places so wild and brimming with life. The only sour note comes from the discovery that we've used our last piece of moleskin. We dare not swim, despite the lure of the water. If the padding that covers our deep blisters peels, hiking out of this remote spot might prove impossible.

After dark, loons deliver a concert of trills and wails. I pad the mossy ground to the water's edge to get an earful and nearly step on a frog. It's five or six inches long, green, and spotted. As I bend over for a close look, my nose wrinkles. This is, I realize, a mink frog, an amphibian of northern wetlands that gives off the sour, urine-like bouquet of a mink. Back at the lean-to, I float into a deep easy sleep while listening to loons and the soft, distant barking of barred owls.

Jim and I limp out of the West Canada Lakes Wilderness the next morning, hiking by way of the banks of the Cedar River. Along the trail, we pause to identify trees—red spruce, white spruce, red pine, white pine, sugar maple, American beech, white birch, and yellow birch—and to talk with an old man who greets us with a loud "Halloo!" He is red-faced and white-haired, nearing eighty, and dressed in a uniform of dark-green shirt and trousers. On his back perches an old-fashioned Adirondack pack basket, worn smooth and stained by age. He tells us about the big blow-down of 1950, waving his hand at the rotting evidence that still makes bushwhacking difficult here, and about the Boy Scouts he is leading to the lean-to we just vacated. We part, and a few minutes later two fortyish men and a group of boys appear, drenched in sweat, struggling to keep up.

A year passes. During it, I scheme to get back to the West Canadas. This time I aim to give the wilderness the homage it deserves—no rushing, no blisters, no overarching plan to hike all the way to Lake Placid. I'll stay a while and let the woods creep into my soul.

In July, I return by way of the Cedar River trail. A naturalist friend, Jeff Main, and I drive in from Indian Lake to the Cedar River Flow. There we climb into a canoe and paddle up the lake several miles until it dwindles into its main feeder stream, which we ascend. When we spy a trail marker on the right bank, we beach the boat, haul it deep into a tangle of blackberry where we hope no thief will find it, and set off on foot. The sky is blue and bright, the air cool. On a narrow track, we plunge into a wet, mossy forest of maple and birch and cross the invisible border into the wilderness.

It's Saturday, and about dinnertime, we arrive at the Cedar Lakes. To our dismay the lean-tos are occupied, the lakes echo with human voices, and the woods abound with tents and people. We decide to rough it and sleep under the stars. At first this proves a fine idea, and we lie awake for hours hypnotized by the stars. But halfway through the night rain begins to fall. Neither of us has the presence of mind to pitch a tent, so I fish a tarp from my pack and pull it over our sleeping bags. By morning the rain has stopped, our faces are well washed, and everything is soggy—the woods, the ground, our gear, our spirits. We struggle to our feet, light a camp stove, and soon have breakfast cooking.

By evening—it's Sunday now, and people are heading home—the woods have emptied and the lakes are ours alone. For two days we lounge, swim, lounge some more, sleep, nap, explore the woods around the lakes, catch mink frogs, study the stars at night, and botanize. Among the trees here are white and red spruce, white and yellow birch, balsam fir, and an array of prospective successors—sugar maple seedlings and beech saplings. On the forest floor, we find clumps of wood ferns, great billowing patches of hay-scented fern, and a dazzling array of mosses. The wet places bristle with carnivorous sundews and pitcher plants. Sunny areas glow brightly with tall sprigs of fireweed.

The whole place teems with birds. Juncos rattle in every bush. Near our shelter a great blue heron, tall as a second grader and just as single-minded, stalks frogs. Song sparrows belt out snatches of Beethoven, waxwings and swallows dart for flies over the water, a raven chortles from the pinnacle of a balsam, and loons fly, paddle, and dive.

In the end, the loons gain the greatest share of my interest. The other birds I can see nearly anywhere, but loons thrive only on big, wild water, and nowhere have I seen them more sumptuously at home than here on the West Canadas. By day, they float regally in the blue-green waters near our shelter, turning like weathervanes with every breeze, laughing when the mood strikes, diving after fish, and launching themselves on reconnaissance flights. By night, they cry and wail as if the world were ending.

On the morning we pack to leave I watch a loon come down like a floatplane. As it rockets in at an acute angle, its feet rake the smooth water into furrows. The belly makes contact, friction overcomes momentum, and the great northern diver (as the English call it) plows slowly to a halt. The loon shakes its head, rears out of the water to stretch its wings, and settles down to drift.

The loon will stay, at least until autumn ice drives it south and coastward, but we must go. I shoulder my pack, making silent MacArthurian resolutions about returning, and follow

Jeff into the woods. One day, I vow, I will make long visits here every month or two through an entire year and deepen my acquaintance.

Ralph Waldo Emerson, a one-time Adirondack visitor, celebrated what he called "the true harmony of the unshorn landscape with horrid thickets and bold mountains and the balance of the land." Leaving the West Canadas, I understand the harmony Emerson found in wild places and feel its tonic, restorative effect on me. I arrived harried and divided, a working man ruled by the clock. I leave serene and whole, a wanderer in a universe beyond time. Inside my psyche, after long happy days of stretching muscles, exercising senses, and living the kind of life for which nature itself designed me, I savor a balance between the wild animal nature that brought me here and the civilized social nature that drives me home.

Burroughs and the Boreas

Mosquitoes swarm in a hypodermic fog, and rain drills us from above. It's hard to gain much pleasure from the place we have come to see—a wild, rarely visited corner of the Adirondacks south of Newcomb, north of Minerva, and west of a cold, blackwater river called, after the Greek name for the North Wind, the Boreas. On we trudge, hauling ourselves up a steep, trailless slope crowded with living and fallen trees.

My wife, Debbie, and I are retracing a journey made in 1863 by John Burroughs (1837-1921), author of some twenty-seven books, friend and mentor of Theodore Roosevelt, and the most celebrated American naturalist of his time.

From a quiet stretch of the Boreas known as the Stillwater, we climb steadily. The forest is lush with shrubs and ferns, their leaves glistening with rain. A stream cascades through troughs and waterfalls toward the river, and its roar drowns out the sound of our footsteps. Ahead and 500 feet above us lies Grassy Pond, our immediate destination.

A few giant sugar maples, yellow birches, and eastern hemlocks tower overhead. These trees, surely well more than a century old, likely shaded Burroughs and his three companions when they tramped here in 1863. Then, loggers had already cleared this part of the Adirondack Park-to-be, but on steep rocky slopes like this one, big trees sometimes escaped the ax and saw. Burroughs spent the night before his climb in a "dilapidated lumberman's shanty," suggesting that the logging had ceased some years earlier.

Debbie and I are here on a day trip, aiming to see a little of what the twenty-six-year-old Burroughs encountered during an adventure that proved pivotal for him. Before his Adirondack visit, this son of the Catskills, raised on a dairy farm, had been a young man of uncertain interests and middling prospects. Yet Burroughs walked out of the woods a changed man. In the months that followed, he would display the qualities that carried him to distinction and fame: ambition, a keen intellect, a passion for nature, and a gift for writing eloquent, evocative prose.

Burroughs's first natural history book, *Wake-Robin* (1871), would not be published for another eight years. (It contains "Adirondac," an essay recounting his camping trip.) A celebrated life as America's foremost literary naturalist, and friendships with Walt Whitman, Theodore Roosevelt, John Muir, and Thomas Edison, lay in the future. Most recently, Burroughs had been teaching school at Buttermilk Falls, a Hudson Valley hamlet south of Albany. He had just met one of his heroes, Ralph Waldo Emerson, taken up botany as a hobby, and rekindled a childhood enthusiasm for birds. Tired of the classroom, Burroughs was eager to re-invent himself.

Debbie and I reached the Stillwater by much the same route Burroughs had followed. For us the journey was made easier by an abandoned Delaware and Hudson railway line, built in 1942 to carry ore from open-pit mines at Tahawus.

Eight miles south of Newcomb on Route 28N, we parked the car and set off along the rails at nine o'clock in the morning.

"When I went to the Adirondacs [sic], which was in the summer of 1863," Burroughs wrote, "I was in the first flush of my ornithological studies, and was curious, above all else, to know what birds I should find in these solitudes." He saw or heard most of the species that we noted while advancing from railroad tie to railroad tie—white-throated sparrows, cedar waxwings, American robins, black-throated blue warblers, hermit thrushes, and more. We recognize birds by their voices, but Burroughs, not yet the expert ornithologist he would become, depended on seeing them.

Burroughs was intrigued by whistles and traced them to a white-throated sparrow. He found the song "very delicate and plaintive." Ubiquitous in the region and prone to carol at all hours, this bird is, at least in my thinking, the voice of the Adirondacks. We hear it, too. The whistled notes have the cadence of someone saying, *Old Sam Peabody-Peabody-Peabody.*

Another bird Burroughs saw was the passenger pigeon, extinct since 1914 but still numerous in 1863. He saw a lone pigeon early in the trek, and later, after he and his camp mates had mounted the ridge, noted that "wild pigeons were quite numerous."

In this early stage of his career, Burroughs often collected the birds he found. Conservation laws were nonexistent, and without the high-quality binoculars we now take for granted, the only way to get a good look at a bird was often to shoot it. Later in life, Burroughs would recant and change his ways. But on this expedition he killed (and presumably ate for dinner) eight spruce grouse—a rare species in the Adirondack

Mountains today. He felled a sharp-shinned hawk, too, after seeing it chase passenger pigeons.

Aside from birds, Debbie and I find a few warty American toads still-hunting for bugs, dozens of eastern garter snakes sunning on railroad ties, and a massive female snapping turtle laying eggs. Dragonflies and butterflies stir the air. The day grows hot and bright. A gauzy haze—ozone pollution, something Burroughs never had to contend with—blurs the trees on the far side of the river. We walk six miles, reaching the Stillwater at noon.

Debbie and I crave rest. But a breeze kicks up, and the tops of the trees sway ominously as if a thunderstorm approaches. Our aim is to find a stream that feeds into the Boreas just downstream of the Stillwater and follow it to ponds Burroughs described. Pausing only to swig some water, we pick our way across a beaver dam and begin to ascend.

Bushwhacking involves a certain amount of danger, especially in a remote place such as this. We have taken precautions. We carry a map, compass, and first-aid kit. Friends have a detailed description of our whereabouts, and they will send help if we fail to return. Thrashing through dense woods up a steep slope, harried by mosquitoes and strafed by rain, we know the importance of being careful. There are better places to sprain an ankle.

"Our journey commenced in a steep and rugged ascent, which brought us," Burroughs wrote, "after an hour's heavy climbing, to an elevated region of pine forest, years before ravished by lumbermen, and presenting all manner of obstacles to our awkward and encumbered pedestrianism." For us, progress and conditions are similar. An hour's sweaty effort delivers us to the same "elevated region." Fallen trunks and limbs and dense live growth loom as thickly as they did in 1863.

Finally we reach a shallow lake, fringed by grassy sedges and reflecting the pewter color of the sky. This is Grassy Pond, known to Burroughs as "Bloody Moose Pond." A moose, he learned, had been slaughtered there some years before his arrival.

"Looking out over the silent and lonely scene," Burroughs and his companions saw something they took for a deer. "As we were eagerly awaiting some movement to confirm this impression, it lifted up its head, and lo! a great blue heron." By happy coincidence, we, too, see a great blue heron. We're pleased to think that the bird might be directly descended from the one Burroughs spied 137 years earlier.

It's 2:30. Debbie and I are exhausted. We've hiked seven miles, the last mile up a rugged slope while we're under constant assault from mosquitoes. We can't rest. The bugs—we curse them now—threaten to drain us of blood. What to do? The woods ahead look impossible to penetrate, at least without a bulldozer. If we force our way through to Nate's Pond, where Burroughs's guide fashioned a jack-light from three candles and birch-bark and helped the naturalist slay a deer, we'll have to turn around the moment we get there. The trek back to Grassy Pond and the tricky off-trail descent to the Boreas still lie ahead, and so do six miles of walking the railroad tracks back to the car. Rubbery knees and failing light increase the risk we'll hurt ourselves.

So we do the sensible thing. We turn back. From this point John Burroughs marched on to Nate's Pond and a deserted village near an old iron mine. In the years that followed, he would write more than two dozen books on nature and philosophy.

Widely celebrated in his lifetime but unsung today, Burroughs played a leading role in awakening readers all over the world to the joys of nature and the importance of living simply. He was never politically active like his friend John Muir, nor did he produce a book-length masterpiece like Henry Thoreau's *Walden*. Yet Burroughs, who wrote magnetically and enjoyed greater commercial success than any nature writer before or since, made more converts to nature appreciation than anyone else, as Paul Brooks argues in *Speaking For Nature* (1980). "They and their successors," writes Brooks, "have been fighting our conservation battles ever since."

Without the influence of Burroughs, public support for the creation of the Adirondack Park in the nineteenth century might have never solidified. In New York State, one famous contemporary, the prominent intellectual Elbert Hubbard (1856–1915), insisted that Burroughs almost alone deserved the credit for stirring public interest in conservation. His role in the park's creation was indirect, but vital.

"Better than fish or game or grand scenery...is the wordless intercourse with rude Nature one has on these expeditions," Burroughs wrote in concluding his story. "It is something to press the pulse of our old mother by mountain lakes and streams, and know what health and vigor are in her veins...."

Debbie and I agree. Tired and sore, we shuffle out of the woods cheered by cedar waxwings that trill softly in alders along the river, and delighted by a mahogany-colored wood turtle that blinks up at us as we gaze into its gold-flecked eyes.

II. WILDLIFE CLOSE TO HOME

Getting to Know
the Neighbors

This is a story about a couple, a pair of naturalists, who roamed the world seeking paradise and found it in the northern Adirondacks. Then, taking a lesson from Milton (not the guy who plows your driveway, but John Milton, the English classical poet), they decided they'd better do something to make sure their paradise never got lost. But what, and how?

The two naturalists were—are—my wife, Debbie, and me. Paradise consisted of eighteen-and-a-half mossy, gently sloping acres in the Adirondack township of St. Armand, near Bloomingdale. In the middle of the property sat a charming but decrepit "camp," or summer place. Its roof leaked, its floors sagged ominously as you walked over them, and the attic contained enough mouse droppings to fill a claw-foot bathtub.

As you might imagine, the selling point was not the house, despite its antique charm. It was the land and its wildlife. The property included upland, lowland, a brook, riverbank, hardwoods, softwoods, and swamp. A quiet dead-end road traversed it north to south, and a river, the Saranac, poured across from west to east. State land abutted the property on one side. The river offered swimming, fishing, and transportation.

We could—and did, once—canoe home from Saranac Lake when the car broke down.

Another selling feature: the northern border of the McKenzie Mountain Wilderness Area, which incorporates 37,620 wild and woolly acres, lay a five minute stroll from the mailbox. We could bushwhack straight to Lake Placid, bustling home of the 1932 and 1980 Winter Olympic Games, without setting foot on a beaten path and meeting only bears and beavers. From the rocky heights of the wilderness, the summit of Moose Mountain gazed down a landslide scar at us. In the distance, away to the south and east, rose the angular profile of a grander mountain named Whiteface.

We bought the place. Instantly we faced two daunting challenges. One was making the camp livable, year-round. The other was, and is, our focus here. How to live on this heavenly patch of *terra firma* without messing it up? We're naturalists, after all. Naturalists worry about that kind of thing.

From the first day we tramped the property with Sandy Hayes, the real estate agent who sold it to us, we could almost feel the plants and animals and the rest of the wild things eyeing us with concern. Even under the protections afforded by Adirondack Park Agency (APA) regulations, we were buying a license to kill and dispose—to fell trees, bulldoze wildflowers, churn up places where toads hibernate, drive the mice out of the house, and an awful lot more. We'd seen what other people do with land, and often we'd been critical. Could we do better?

Into the muddle fell a ray of light. It was an idea, a plan for inhabiting the place in as gentle a way possible, a plan that would go a long way toward guaranteeing that the flora, fauna, fungi, and microbial life of the property could keep on enjoying life, liberty, and the pursuit of happiness. After all, my own Adirondack ancestors, among the first pioneers here, go back merely a couple of hundred years. Theirs go back millennia. What gave us the right to move in and make the lives of wild things miserable, or to displace them? All we had was a piece of paper—one with legal standing, but of shaky moral foundation.

Our goal was to live in some sort of harmony with the life already thriving on the property. But how to accomplish it? We decided the best way to start would be to launch a biological survey, one that would demand much of us and never really be finished. We'd attempt to identify every living thing. Only by learning what we had, we reckoned, could we ensure that nothing, no piece of our paradise, was lost thoughtlessly.

If the idea sounds original, I confess it isn't. Organizations such as The Nature Conservancy are forever conducting biological inventories, and I myself once organized a team of professional and amateur biologists to survey the wildlife of a 4,700-acre county park, back in the 1980s. Perhaps you keep lists yourself. But this was something new and exciting for us: getting to know the woody trees and shrubs and soft-stemmed wildflowers, ferns and mosses, mammals and birds, reptiles and amphibians, and more with which we shared a home. With them we intended to share paradise for the rest of our days.

Feeling daunted by the immensity of the task, and hungering for inspiration, we thought back to Frank Lutz. In 1941, Lutz was serving as Curator of Insects at the American Museum of Natural History in New York. He had lobbied his boss for more assistants, arguing that there were three times as many kinds of insects as other kinds of animals, therefore three-fourths of the museum's zoologists ought to be entomologists. The Director refused to be convinced. Lutz countered with a proposition. He would count the insects on his 75-by-200-foot lot in suburban New Jersey. There, he boasted, he could tally 500 species with little trouble. For every species he identified beyond 500, Lutz wanted a ten-dollar-a-year raise. If he fell short of 500, he would welcome a ten dollar per species pay cut.

As it happened, the boss refused to play. Just for fun, Lutz went ahead anyhow. By the time he was done, he had scoured his ecologically compromised third of an acre and found 1,402 species! Every one was a kind of insect. There were, to cite a few highlights, 167 kinds of bees and wasps, 467 species of moths and butterflies, 258 types of fly, and 259 varieties of beetle. One bee was a tropical species never before found north of the West Indies. Unfortunately, Lutz's $9,020 raise never materialized. But the story of the chase was immortalized in a classic of nature writing, *A Lot Of Insects*.

If Frank Lutz could find 1,402 insect species on a close-cropped quarter acre, what might exist on our spread in the Adirondacks? The mind boggled. Of course, we're not the entomologists that Lutz was, and species diversity drops in cold climates. Yet we intended to survey not just insects. We set our sights on all five of the kingdoms into which modern biologists divide life: the bacteria, the protoctists (including protozoa and algae), the animals, the fungi, and the plants. The task was Herculean. The only thing to do was to approach it calmly and with resolve, like one confronts a mountain. We'd take one step at a time.

So we were off. The mortgage papers weren't even signed yet on the day in late winter when we made our first scientific expedition to the property. The weather was cold and gray, and a thermometer inside the house registered near zero. But this was an august occasion. With a notepad tucked into a pocket in my down jacket, Debbie and I trudged across the lawn and into the woods. Soon we were recording our first discoveries:

Black-capped chickadee
Common raven
Hairy woodpecker
Whitetail deer (tracks and scat)
Balsam fir
White pine
Eastern hemlock
Tamarack
Northern white-cedar
Red spruce
White birch
Red maple
Quaking aspen
Black cherry
American beech
Speckled alder
Beaked hazelnut
Hobblebush
Red-osier dogwood

Those were our first records. We also found droppings left by a grouse. Although we felt certain they were the work of the ruffed grouse, known in the Adirondacks as the partridge, the boggy habitat of the rare spruce grouse lies close at hand. The honest thing to do, the scientific thing, was to leave ruffed grouse off the list until the evidence was certain. That's the way we'd play the game.

We couldn't move into the house until the weather warmed. It had no heat source. Until the first of May we were visitors, driving out at every opportunity from an apartment in Saranac Lake to push ahead with the survey. By the end of March, our bird list had grown to nine species. We confirmed the presence of ruffed grouse on the place by seeing one, and we'd observed an American crow, a pileated woodpecker, and several mallard ducks. As skilled bird watchers, we could also enlarge the list through the evidence of our ears. The end of March brought the giggling of the season's first American robin and the wing-whistling and *peent* call of an American woodcock.

As the snow melted, the worrisome condition of the house became increasingly apparent. April Fool's Day brought dark thoughts, a feeling that the joke was on us. But was it? A morning visit to Moose Hill Farm, as we'd decided to call the place, relieved us of gloom. We saw six new birds! The Adirondack spring was barely underway, and already the place was revealing a wealth of bird life.

Our lists grew by leaps and bounds. By the end of April, we'd recorded forty-two species of birds on the property. At the end of another week, we had fifty-seven, and by month's end, the tally had climbed to seventy-eight. Number seventy-eight was a stunner: a blazing orange Blackburnian warbler, singing from the top of a tree. The fact that this bird had migrated from a forest somewhere in South America to our home turf in the Adirondacks pleased us no end.

Every naturalist has subject areas regarding which he knows a great deal, and others in which he admits himself an ignoramus. So it was with Debbie and me. We were making big strides in identifying vertebrate animals (mammals, birds, reptiles, amphibians) and vascular plants (ones with "plumbing"), but in other areas progress was sorely lacking. We had named no mosses, which are non-vascular plants, identified only a paltry few insects, and not keyed out a single bacterium, fungus, or protoctist. The message was clear. We'd have to work extra hard in these areas, and it would be sensible to recruit outside help.

That summer, as we labored to replace rotten beams and floor joists, dig foundation drains, and install a winterized water supply, our biological survey work slowed. Yet advances came. One morning, a new mammal was added to the lists when I was working in the old bedroom that had become my office, and a masked shrew walked in. Hardly larger in body size than a bumblebee, with a tail the thickness of pencil lead, it emerged from under a closet door, patrolled the room's perimeter while twitching cinnamon-colored whiskers, and disappeared back where it came from.

That wasn't the only in-house wildlife sighting. There was a steady stream of mice, including two unlucky ones that drowned in a wastebasket we'd positioned under a roof-leak. The corpses allowed us to confirm that the mice were deer mice, *Peromyscus maniculatus,* and not white-footed mice, *P. leucopus.* Deer mice have long bristles extending beyond the cartilaginous parts of their tails. White-footed mice do not.

Inside the house, we saw a red squirrel once, and twice in the bathtub there were pseudoscorpions. If you have never had the pleasure of meeting a pseudoscorpion, think small. The entire animal, an arachnid distantly related to spiders and genuine scorpions, could fit with room to spare on your thumbnail. It is a creature of the forest floor, where it roams the leaf litter using pincer-like claws to capture fellow invertebrates. Occasionally pseudoscorpions turn up in moist places in houses. They are fun to observe and not at all dangerous.

Highlights of our survey's first year included two visits from experts who volunteered to lend a hand. The first was Wayne Gall, then Curator of Insects at the Buffalo Museum of Science. On the evening of August 23, he hung a white bed sheet on our property near the river and illuminated it with a black light. Wayne is a superb all-round naturalist, but he specializes in caddisflies. These are insects with hairy, diaphanous wings that they hold over their backs like a tent. As we watched in awe, insects flooded out of the darkness onto the sheet. From among them, Wayne collected forty-seven caddisflies. Months later, he identified them back at the museum. Eight species could be named with certainty, he said, including one so wide-ranging that it has also been recorded in Hawaii.

Our second expert visitor was Edwin Ketchledge, the dean of Adirondack naturalists, retired after a long and distinguished career on the faculty of the SUNY Environmental Science and Forestry school in Syracuse. "Ketch" is an expert botanist, and he agreed to look over our property for mosses. One fall day we tromped around. Ketch rattled off names, and I scribbled them in a notebook. Occasionally he'd trumpet the praises of a particular patch of moss, or grumble that he couldn't recall a scientific name. By the end of the walk, he had recorded eight moss species with certainty and several more that could be named with further study. The prettiest was a leafy, extravagant moss called *Hylocomnium splendens,* and the most unexpected, said Ketch, was *Neckera pennata,* usually found in old-growth forest. The logged-over woods we had purchased was a surprising place to find it.

Happily, our construction projects sometimes complemented our biological work. One day when I was examining an old water pump with an eye toward replacing it, I spied our first reptile, a garter snake. A trench dug by a backhoe, leading more than 150 feet from the well to the house, proved a handy device for live-trapping additional garter snakes, and it caught American toads, too. They'd fall into the ditch at night, and every morning we'd collect them in a bucket and set them free.

There were a few tragedies. Once, in a waterlogged crawl space beneath a bedroom, we spotted a moss that seemed to glow in the dark. Sometime later, in the midst of struggling with building materials, the spot where the moss grew was disturbed and the plant obliterated. I asked Ketch if it could be a species of luminous moss that I'd heard about. "*Schistostega pennata,*" he said. "It probably was." Most of our bad luck involved animals drowned in rainwater that had accumulated in buckets. We lost a beloved half-tame chipmunk that way, and also several mice and voles.

Since the idea was not only to study the property's wild things, but also to make sure they had safe homes, we moved forward on other fronts, too. We began ridding the house of mice, not by killing them, but by patching the holes where they got in and escorting them outside in live traps. We also stopped mowing the lawn. There is nothing Adirondack about a close-cropped expanse of grass, so why have one? Most of the grasses hail from Europe and Asia, and a lawn offers little food or shelter for wildlife. Responses were immediate. Neighbors began to raise eyebrows. Bird activity increased dramatically. Small mammals proliferated—outside, where they belonged. Mosquitoes, alas, multiplied. Almost overnight, a dull carpet of green metamorphosed into a dazzling crazy quilt of wildflowers.

By the end of the first year, our efforts had produced species lists that were by no means comprehensive, yet they represented a good start. Knowledge, actually a lack of it, had limited us, and time had, too. Nevertheless, we recorded thirteen species of mammals (including black bear, American mink, and a self-introduced primate called the human being), eighty-eight species of birds (among them bald eagle and American bittern), one snake, two turtles, seven frogs, one salamander, twenty-four species of trees, and an array of shrubs and herbs.

Admittedly, there were embarrassing shortfalls. We identified no spiders. We keyed out only a few insects beyond Wayne Gall's caddisflies, and there were no records for crustaceans, snails, freshwater mollusks, leeches, or fish. We had not identified a single alga or bacterium, either, at least until a few days ago. Then I was reading the fine print on a yogurt container we'd just emptied, and voila! Four bacteria in the live culture were named at the species level: *Lactobacillus acidophilus, L. bulgaricus, L. casei,* and *L. reuteri.* Our rule: If it's on the property and it's living, we count it.

A biological survey, if it aims to be comprehensive, must look in all directions, including up, down, out, and in. One day we'll get around to coaxing out a specimen of *Demodex folliculorum,* a tiny mite that lives in human hair follicles. On another occasion, we'll recruit a dermatologist to identify some of the bacteria on our skin. There are gastrointestinal microbes to consider, too, as well as the spiders that festoon our house with cobwebs, the fungi that sprout beneath the vapor barrier we put down in the crawl space, and the lichen that live on the roof. The possibilities are almost endless. We observe everything, and if we can help it, we kill nothing.

So on we go. In the second year of our homesteading odyssey, the survey brought us to unexplored corners of the property and to exciting discoveries. A moose still eludes us, despite the fact that a neighbor saw a handsome bull on the property a year before we bought it. But we added one of the world's few poisonous mammals, the short-tailed shrew, which poses no serious threat to humans but carries a potent neurotoxin in its saliva, and the bird list jumped to 118 species, a respectable tally for the northern Adirondacks. The first bird of 2001 was a predatory songbird called a northern shrike. It spent a couple of January days hunting fellow songbirds around our bird feeders. Last came snow geese, a flock of more than 100, beating the air high overhead. Moving toward the southeast one December afternoon, they remained unobserved until their squawking caught my attention.

The second year also brought a fisher, whose tracks turned up in snow behind the house; a coyote chorus that sang and thrilled us one April night; a northern flying squirrel that began putting in regular nocturnal visits at our bird feeders; a mourning warbler that Debbie chased at six one morning while I remained abed; and a red bat that on November 3 flew figure-eights over the open space formerly known as a lawn. We also made headway with fungi, upping our total from one species (gabled false morel) to seven. Among our favorites were the disgusting-looking but somehow endearing chocolate tube slime, the fetching eyelash cup, and the tinder polypore, a shelf fungus that looks like a horse's hoof. The dry insides of the tinder polypore were once prized by woodsmen for fire-starting. An interesting bit of trivia: Recent discoveries in molecular biology suggest that fungi are more closely related to you, me, and other animals than they are to plants.

Speaking of plants, their numbers in our files mount. We were thrilled to find cardinal-flower blooming on a sandbar along the river. This is a wild lobelia whose blossoms glow a hypnotic, fiery red. We found turtlehead, too, growing across the stream from the cardinal-flower, and we identified our first goldenrods, which wasn't easy because even experts disagree on how to separate one species from the next. The second year of survey work also saw the further renaissance of our late lawn. The two acres or so of meadow not only filled with wildflowers, but butterflies arrived in profusion. Among the new ones we recorded were the spring azure, red-spotted purple, Harris's checkerspot, viceroy, American copper, great spangled fritillary, and American painted lady. We identified several moths, too. One was the Isabella, unknown to most people except in its larval form, the woolly bear caterpillar.

Where from here? Next year, we hope, will see us working on the house a little less, and chasing birds and butterflies a little more. We're eager to persuade an old friend who studies dragonflies to visit this year, and a friend who works as a fisheries biologist has expressed interest in helping fill the most shocking of our gaps. We've named no fish. Neighbors talk of pike in the river, and of bullheads and bass, but to date we've not seen one caught within our property boundaries.

Meanwhile, all the knowledge we're gaining is helping us make informed decisions about what to do with the land. We've identified thickets where birds nest, and we know that fallen tree-trunks, especially toppled balsam firs of a certain size, serve male ruffed grouse as platforms for display. There are standing dead trees that will stay because hawks and olive-sided flycatchers perch on them, woodpeckers and other birds nest inside, and woodpeckers drum on the hollow trunks for mates. We eliminated non-native hydrangeas in front of the house because they interfered with repair projects, but now that we see the importance of the remaining hydrangeas to migrating monarch butterflies, we'll defend the sixty that remain along the driveway.

The beauty of a project such as ours is that anyone can do it, anywhere. Eighteen and a half acres in the northern Adirondacks work fine, yet the idea could easily be transposed to a suburban back yard or a penthouse garden in Manhattan. It helps if you start out with a working knowledge of natural history, but what you don't know, you can learn. Or, as we're beginning to do, one can recruit experts. Good record keeping is vital. Most people today would employ a computer, but as chief data manager for our project, I've opted for old-fashioned file cards. I see too much of a computer screen already. It's a pleasure for me to sit down at a wooden desk and write out survey cards by hand. We store them in old card files I found at a yard sale, and if the power goes off, I can still tell you on what date we saw our first goshawk.

Are we crazy? Perhaps. I have no doubt some of our neighbors think we are. But I can tell you I've never felt so at home in a place, and I know the reason why. It's this: that during the more than two years Debbie and I have worked on our survey, we've forged deep emotional connections with our community—not only with our congenial human neighbors in Bloomingdale and Saranac Lake, but also with all those thousands of non-human others, most of whom we haven't yet identified. With these organisms we share a similar taste in habitat. With them we gladly link our fates.

Rodents of
Mass Destruction

PRELUDE

Squeak-squeak-squeak! My hand recoils, fingertips intact. The sound suggests bats stirred up in an attic. But this is a sock drawer in a first-floor bedroom in a sprawling wooden house in the Adirondacks.

Next, a dark shape steals out of something big and fluffy— I'm not sure at first what I'm seeing. All I know is that a drawer meant to hold only socks contains two unidentified objects, one of them moving, the other the size of a softball.

The moving thing vanishes as soon as I glimpse it. But I've seen enough to name it. The intruder is a deer mouse, *Peromyscus maniculatus* in the lingo of scientists, gray of back, white of belly and feet.

I gaze into the drawer, dumbstruck. Out of the fluffy thing crawls a third surprise, a miniature version of the first. Its eyes have not yet opened on the world, and it gropes its way into a corner.

What on earth is going on? I think for a moment before the obvious becomes clear.

I have two sock drawers, one for socks used daily, the other, in another part of the room, for hiking socks that get occasional use. Not having climbed a mountain in our extended

Adirondack backyard all summer, the second drawer has been sitting idle. Absentmindedly, I've left it open a crack.

"Nature," said Rabelais, "abhors a vacuum."

Enjoying the run of the house despite extensive live-trapping and hole-plugging, the deer mouse must have reconnoitered the drawer and found it a fine vacuum in which to raise a family. So it set to work. Craving material of just the right softness and insulating value to form a nest, it began taking nips out of things at hand—one of my favorite shirts, the sweater I'm wearing as I compose these lines, a tee-shirt, a pajama top. None sufficed. So the mouse kept on trying until it found the perfect resource: the fleece lining of Debbie's Australian-made house slippers.

Bit by bit, the mouse clipped fleece from inside the slippers and ferried it across the room and into the chest of drawers. There in my sock drawer it molded the stuff into a pear-shaped mass, golden, half again as large as a doubled-up pair of hiking socks. Atop the thing it fashioned a hole, giving access to the interior.

What's a naturalist to do? On one hand, I feel an impulse to murder. Here's a chance to strike back at the rodent that has lain waste to my wardrobe. On the other, I look down at the baby and the cluster of fuzzy siblings I find cuddled in the nest. No, I cannot kill these mice. I will not kill these mice. The offspring are innocent of all crimes, although I can guess the mayhem they're destined for. A solution comes to mind. I'll relocate them to our utility shed, resigned to the fact that my forbearance will come back to haunt me.

The trick is moving Mama and babies together. Without maternal attentions, the little ones will shiver and starve. I pluck up the errant mousling and plunk it back in the nest. Then I bait a live trap with peanut butter and raisins and wedge it inside the drawer. Turning off the overhead light, I retreat to the living room.

A half hour later, the trap snaps. Success! I hurry to the scene. An indignant Mama Mouse rattles inside the trap.

My wife, Debbie, supplies a shoebox. Inside it, we put the former lining of her slippers, animate contents included. Carrying the box and the trap, I set off for the shed. It's a cold winter night. My breath forms a cloud in the moonlight.

In a corner near a roto-tiller, I wedge the box where it cannot fall. Then I open the trap. Mother Mouse pokes out her nose, wiggles her exquisitely sensitive whiskers, and sniffs the opening of the nest. At exactly that moment, I shake the trap. Mama lands inside the nest with her babies.

I switch off the light and flee. How do I feel about the whole thing? Emotions are mixed. The most widespread North American rodent has nearly the entire continent to choose from, yet it picks my sock drawer as the place to raise its young. I'm flattered, yet angry, too. Debbie is short a favorite pair of slippers, and I'm not over the sweater and shirts.

THE SEARCH FOR RMD BEGINS

One morning last week at 0900 hours, Operation Mouse commences. It is the latest in a series of efforts designed to rid our Adirondack domicile of rodents of mass destruction (RMD).

The crisis has been years in the making. Mouse droppings resembling grains of wild rice have been turning up just about everywhere: on the kitchen counter, along baseboards, and inside shoes and boxes. Intelligence operatives working inside the house report sightings of mouse-sized, furry objects scooting under the refrigerator and out from under the sofa. The house is old, the interior warm. Winter rages outdoors, and mice can squeeze through all but the tiniest holes.

RMD nibble apples left out in bowls. A sack full of corn kernels, marketed not for consumption but to be heated in a microwave and placed against a sore back, turns up empty. The missing kernels later appear in a closet, tucked neatly inside a boot. All this is mildly annoying beside the chief irritation: ragged holes chewed in shirts and sweaters.

Who is doing the chewing? Larder beetles, tiny banded things notorious for their appetite for textiles, are located and identified. These are known to nibble their way through clothing. But the number of favorite shirts ruined and the combined surface area of the damage seems out of proportion to the tiny size and modest number of the insects.

Central Domestic Intelligence searches the literature. We learn that deer mice are famous for wreaking havoc in fabric. They construct nests with the stuff, and they create insulated bivouacs in which to sleep. In fact, while ripping apart walls in our house, which lacked insulation of any kind when we bought it, we found a few bays between studs filled with soft insulating material. The bays were filled with mouse droppings, too. If we had the patience, we probably could have insulated the entire house by piling cellulose insulation in the middle of each room, then standing back while the rodents tucked it in place.

Years pass. Every likely hole and crack in the perimeter has been sealed. Yet the little sons-and-daughters-of-unwed-mothers keep on coming. Last week, I discovered a new sweater, one I'm fond of, given to me at Christmas, with a hole in it the size of a dessert plate.

That's it, I cried. No more Mr. Nice Guy. This is war. I shall never surrender until our house is rid of RMD once and for all. We will fight the mice in the attic and we will fight them in the crawl space, and we shall drive them from our realm.

On consecutive days, two plain brown packages arrive via special courier. One contains a portable black light. The other holds three jars of fluorescent powder, courtesy of a kind salesman at the DayGlo® corporation, who laughed at my story and offered to send free samples. I borrow my battle plan from Charlotte Demers, a research biologist at the Adirondack Ecological Center. Taking her own methods from biologists who study small mammals in the field, Demers had waged and won a similar campaign against mice plaguing the research station where she works.

At 0900 hours, I remove a frisky mouse from a live trap set the previous evening near our refrigerator. Rather than release the animal directly, I drop it into the depths of a bag containing fluorescent powder—flaming orange, to be exact. After the miscreant has colored itself while searching for a way out of the bag, I set it free outside.

At 2000 hours, I don stealth gear (black turtleneck, dark trousers, etc.), and with black light in hand, plunge through a trapdoor in a hallway into the crawl space. This won't be a happy adventure. I'm mildly claustrophobic, but at least I'm not afraid of spiders.

I have hopes of immediate triumph, of seeing a telltale orange glow linking the hole that lets mice into the crawl space to the one providing egress to the world of shirts and sweaters above. But after a half hour of sleuthing, they're dashed. I find nothing. So I climb out, shut off the lights in the house room by room, and scan every seam for DayGlo® orange.

No luck here, either.

I try the procedure a second time, keeping the mouse captive all day, then releasing it late at night. RMD in our house are most active at night. I hope the insurgent will return at once, tracing a luminescent path to the kitchen counter faster than I can say "significant combat operations have been concluded."

Alas, I fail again.

In the middle of the ensuing night, a call of nature wakes me, and I'm alerted to a trap rattling beside the fridge. Desperate for victory, I try again. At 0300 hours or thereabouts, a third fluorescent mouse vanishes into the night.

Tonight, I'll switch on the black light, head down under, and see what I find.

THE SEARCH FOR RMD CONTINUES

Ten Adirondack deer mice lured by peanut butter blunder hungrily into live traps. Ten lucky deer mice go free. (Most homeowners or their cats slaughter the rodents without a second thought.) In each case, between capture and liberty lies a shake in a plastic bag loaded with fluorescent orange powder.

Out come the mice, blazing like campfires. One by one, over the course of several days, they scurry into the night, generally beginning their adventures on the far side of the color line by darting beneath our mudroom. Twice, mice shoot through a gap in our house's foundation right before my eyes. The gap is so small I can't fit a finger in it.

Down in the crawl space, evidence of rodents of mass destruction grows plain to see. I wriggle down there in pitch darkness, brushing away spider webs, fiddling with a newly purchased battery-powered blacklight that has already developed a loose connection. The eerie purple light flickers on. Then it goes out, plunging me and the spiders that inhabit the crawl space by the hundred back into velvet blackness.

Eventually I gain a measure of mastery over the light's quirks and begin a foundation tour. At first I find nothing. The purple glow makes the words and numbers printed on PVC sewer pipes light up, but the orange trails I've come seeking are nowhere to be found.

But then—Aha! A tunnel through insulation tucked against the house's band joist (a sort of waistband around the framing that holds up the floor) flares a menacing orange, like a live coal. The location matches a known breach in the foundation. A suspicion is confirmed: despite various slapdash efforts to close foundation gaps, RMD are penetrating our lower perimeter.

Now things turn fun. From the hole, I trace pencil-thin smears of orange that mark the passage of one or more mice. They run along a floor joist, onto the broad surface of a hemlock beam, down the beam to another point on the perimeter, and into a second orange hole. As best I can tell, the opening leads nowhere. But I plan to keep an eye on it.

The more I search, the more wisps of orange glare back at me from the darkness. I spy places where mice have followed pipes in search of passage through the floor above. I find a virtual Jackson Pollack of orange around our hot water heater, which is wrapped in glass-wool insulation. RMD have been mining the stuff, probably for nest linings.

Upstairs, I mount a parallel search. Room by room, I shut off lights, switch on the ultraviolet, and scan. Nothing. But on a second pass, more thorough than the first, I find what I seek. Orange powder sparkles beneath the kitchen cooking range, along the tops of bookcases, and up one side of a massive fieldstone fireplace. To my surprise, several mouse-sized holes I've suspected to be entry points are blank.

I focus my attentions on the fireplace. If I'm not mistaken, a glimmer of orange appears in a narrow gap between cove molding and a billion-year-old granite boulder. This may be the proverbial smoking gun: the portal through which buck-toothed, clothing-chewing *Peromyscus maniculatus* are penetrating our personal space. The next day, I fill the gap and others around the masonry, inside the house and outside, with foam insulation extruded from a can. The hardened foam may not hold off mice forever, but if it stops the influx even for a week or two, our Department of Home Security will gain valuable intelligence.

Does it work? In the nights that follow, I catch several more mice. None are colored orange. None excretes orange droppings. Apparently, powdered mice liberated outside aren't getting in. Then why aren't we mouse-free?

It occurs to me while lying awake one night that entire generations of mice might pass their lives inside our comfortable sanctuary without ever venturing outside. Why bother? There's food and soft bedding aplenty, and predators are scarce. Debbie adds support to the theory of permanent resident aliens while moving a chair in the living room. Tilting it, she hears an avalanche of small objects clatter to one side. Shifting the chair in another direction, the avalanche repeats itself. From a gap in the upholstery beneath the seat quantities of two recognizable items trickle out: sunflower seeds and corn kernels. A mouse's pantry! And it's better stocked than our own.

Is the battle won, or has the enemy merely been engaged? Stay tuned.

WE DECLARE VICTORY, SORT OF

By this time, I have been engaged for several months in a battle against Rodents of Mass Destruction (RMD). Deer mice have enjoyed the run of our Adirondack house since it was built in 1922. Futile though one of my neighbors asserts the effort will prove to be, I've made it my mission since the beginning of February to drive the Pendleton-shirt-chewing rodents once and for all from our closets, from our furniture, off our kitchen counters, and out of our bedroom.

One night, minutes after falling asleep, I jolt awake at 11:30 p.m. In the kitchen, an aluminum box trap has snapped shut. Grumbling, I wrench myself out of bed, shuffle down the hall, carry the trap outside into the dark, cold night, and shake its contents into a plastic bag generously supplied with orange powder. Seconds later, a fluorescent orange deer mouse darts away.

Then back to bed, but not for long. The sequence is repeated around 2:30 a.m. and again at 4:30. This goes on for nearly three months—not every night, but several nights a week. I start with orange powder, shift to blue after a few weeks, and end with lemon-yellow. The dozens of mice I catch are released in the same spot, a patch of lawn, now rainbow-colored, just outside the porch door.

For all my troubles, this is what I've learned. RMD have entry holes in the bedroom, the bathroom, the living room, and in a closet in my office. They penetrate holes in studs and plates left open by plumbers and electricians (I'm one of the guilty parties), they squeeze between gaps in floorboards, and they wedge themselves, in the manner of rock climbers scaling the kind of geologic formation called a chimney, up and out the slender gap between a door jamb and stud. I marvel at their ingenuity. Such explorers! Year after year, it seems, RMD probe a structure, seeking every tiny gap, never discouraged, constantly on the lookout for new routes to the resources they seek.

With cement, hardware cloth, foam insulation, sheet metal, and carefully measured bits of wood, I close rodent entrances one by one. Each time, I set traps afterward, hopeful I'll find them empty in the morning. Each time, mice rattling in traps awaken me at 11:30, 2:30, and 4:30, or thereabouts. Just when I think I've found the last portal, the mice prove they have another.

Our most regular customer, the rodent we curse the most often and loudly, comes to be nicknamed the Stove Mouse. It lives in our kitchen cooking range, stealing in at the bottom and sometimes popping out at the top. The space between the stove's inner workings and it's outer shell is stuffed with insulation, and this makes a fine mouse house. The kitchen reeks of fermented rodent pee every time we use the oven. Heat drives the mouse out and nearly drives us out, too, yet the Stove Mouse always comes back after the metal has cooled.

After one more hole-plugging, we catch the Stove Mouse and release it. Days pass. Can it be? No mice! No mice! We set traps, but I sleep undisturbed and in the morning, they're empty.

I'm weary of fluorescent powder and middle-of-the-night research. I'd like to claim we've won the battle. Have we? Yes and no.

In the driveway, something has been invading our Toyota sedan, pulling tissues from a box of Kleenex and chewing them to bits. What's more, this morning, I noticed a telltale scats under the dish drying rack in the kitchen.

Proof of RMD? I pretend they're not there and claim, as Nixon and Kissinger once did, victory and "peace with honor." Yet I know the story is not yet over.

RODENTS OF
MASS DESTRUCTION STRIKE BACK

There were hints, but the clearest proof that Rodents of Mass Destruction are back in our lives comes one afternoon in a supermarket parking lot. There, my wife pops open the trunk of our Toyota Camry, and out springs a bug-eyed mouse. Being a realist, Debbie knows there are more rodents where this one comes from.

So there are. In the days and weeks that follow, the mice we hoped we had driven from our Adirondack house demonstrate that they have negated all our efforts to locate and plug their crawlways. Morale sags. Not only are RMD more abundant than ever and back to their old tricks, but they've rubbed salt in their triumph by taking over our car.

At first, the mice confine their little black droppings to the Toyota's trunk. But these are Marco Polos and Amelia Earharts of the animal world. Before long, they've explored their way into the passenger compartment. Ned, our two-year-old son, leaves crumbs in his car seat. These are the riches the adventurers, which weigh an ounce apiece, intend to exploit.

A new campaign calls for a twist on old tactics. I decide to turn our former stratagem on its head, and rather than catch mice indoors, dunk them in fluorescent powder, and release them outside, I will liberate the glittering captives inside. Afterward, I'll do my best to terrorize the mice to flee straight for their entry-and-exit holes. This will involve risk. The mice may smear colored powder all over our furniture and carpets. Still, because the mice are almost certain to travel directly to their crawlways, the gamble seems worth taking.

We test the technique on the porch. At first, closing off every possible entry hole with wood, glue, and nails seems only to increase the sightings and spoor. But a single mouse, powdered orange and dumped on the floor, leads us in seconds to a gaping hole we've somehow overlooked. Over the years, the porch has slumped a little, opening up a breach the mice have located and exploited.

I close it with wedges of wood. For the first time in ages, I'm feeling optimistic.

Now I shift the campaign indoors. In the living room one night, I trap a second mouse. This one I powder yellow before setting it free on our fieldstone fireplace. I've gone to great lengths to close all possible gaps where the stone meets the walls, yet I suspect the mice still have a fireside entryway.

I'm wrong. The yellow mouse hopscotches across the stones, then drops to the floor and scurries along a baseboard. Its journey leads from the living room, across a pine threshold, and into a bathroom. There the mouse vanishes before Debbie's eyes. She feels certain it dove into a small and hitherto undiscovered gap in the woodwork that frames a shower stall. I sprawl on the floor and twist my neck. Eureka! I spy an opening that gleams like a waxed lemon.

This morning, I close the hole with wood, glue, nails, and, for good measure, a piece of galvanized iron. That's where we stand. No mouse has visited the porch since my last effort there, so we harbor hopes that our lives may at last be rodent-free.

But I'm not making any bets.

EPILOGUE

In the house at night, all is quiet save for the clamor and loon-like laughter of our two-and-a-half year old son, Ned, careening around the house, and for the pitter-patter and giggles of his nine-month-old baby sister, Tassie, chasing him at a full-throttle crawl. No mouse droppings litter the dish drain beside the kitchen sink. The oven produces heat without odor. The vials of colored powder are put away now, and mousetraps sit idle.

Sometimes I almost miss the mice. But then I switch off the lights in Ned's room and cuddle him to sleep, and as I lie there, I hear incisors gnawing on wood somewhere above the ceiling. The rodents have not given up. They continue to probe, continue to seek out crevices or air currents or slivers of incandescent light that tell them a passageway to untold riches will be theirs if only they enlarge it. I know we have not seen the last of them.

Victory—ephemeral though it may prove—came after two pitched battles. The first occurred in the pantry. I was putting something away late one night when my eye caught a shape withdrawing into the shadows on the topmost shelf. It was a lucky sighting. Had I not spied that mouse, hundreds of dollars worth of stored flour, pasta, cookies, crackers, flavored rice mixes, grains, and nuts might have been ruined before we discovered that our perimeter had again been breached. As it was, I spent hours the next morning ripping apart the pantry, discovering extensive but not crushing losses to our food reserves. In an upper corner of the telephone-booth-sized room I found a hole gnawed by RMD, one that gave access to riches beyond a mouse's imagination.

All through the afternoon, I cut heavy sheet metal with tin snips, folded it at right angles, and nailed it up where the walls of the pantry met the ceiling. Then, using a table saw, I ripped strips of wood to reinforce the pantry's corners all the way to the floor. This was a battle we couldn't afford to lose, so I spared no detail.

My efforts succeeded. But the rodents trumped my persistence by finding a slight gap in a laundry closet where a vent pipe pierces the sheetrock of the ceiling on its way into the attic. Hardly had we achieved victory in the pantry than black rice began raining down on the top of our washing machine. "Excrement!" I cried, so to speak. Thus began the final battle.

Hours more went into ripping apart the closet, which in addition to housing a washing machine stores untold useful items such as paint, varnish, duct tape, cleaning solutions, light bulbs, and tubes of caulk. I quickly located the entry hole and nailed over it a few square inches of metal. Two or three nights later, the droppings covered the washer again, and a hole twice as big as the first gaped beside the patch.

"Don't get mad, get even," my father used to tell me. I stalked out to the shed, found a square foot of the thickest, toughest galvanized iron I could find, and attacked it with metal-cutting shears. This time I scribed and cut the metal carefully so it fitted tightly around the vent pipe, and I folded it so that iron spread in all directions around the penetrated corner. It was past midnight when I stood on a stepladder driving in the last nail.

That was it. Our epic conflict ended (at least for the time being) not with a whimper but with the bang of a nail. We hear scratchings and chewings in the night from time to time, but that's all. My sock drawer holds only socks. Debbie's new fleece-lined slippers warm her feet on cold nights, of which in the Adirondacks we have many. New wool shirts hang in my closet, untouched by Rodents of Mass Destruction. Peacetime is good.

The Truth about Snow

Those who visit the Adirondack Mountains from warm places can be forgiven for romanticizing snow. Back home, they hear Christmas songs extolling the joys of Christmases and sleigh rides. They gape at pictures of cottages with snow-covered roofs and think how warm and cozy they would feel if they were inside. Perhaps, too, they remember, or a friend remembers, dear old days when the snow fell thick and deep, life was good, and a January storm meant happy play on skis, sleds, or snowshoes.

What can tropical people (by whom I mean all who live south of Glens Falls) know of snow, really? Imagining the stuff at a distance is like dreaming of future bliss with a lover. The only way to learn snow's true nature, I am certain, is to marry it.

Which is more or less what my wife, Debbie, and I did when we moved to the Adirondacks. The first winter in our house, snow began falling in October and didn't stop until May. All in all, eighteen feet, nearly five and a half meters, fell from the sky. By mid-January, we were shoveling snow off the roofs of the house and shed to keep them from collapsing. We had reason to worry. A neighbor pulled her car out of the garage one morning, and a few minutes later the entire structure, whose roof had not been cleared, went from three dimension to two.

At our house, the heaps created by clearing the roof grew so high that after a while we looked out the windows and saw only a counterscarp of white. By the third week in February, snow had obviated the need for a ladder. To reach the roof, I'd pick the nearest snow pile and walk straight to the peak. About once a week, I'd take a shovel and hack openings to let light in and give us a view outside.

What sort of hell-frozen-over had we gotten ourselves into? The question kept us awake nights.

Not long before our arrival in the Adirondacks, we had been living in Mississippi, on the flat, subtropical coast of the Gulf of Mexico. Snow was so rare that when it piled up like cotton in the interior of the state, our neighbors loaded their children into automobiles and drove north to show them the spectacle.

Those days lie far behind us now. In the Adirondacks, snow isn't something we need to go out of our way to admire.

During this, our third winter in the house, Debbie and I move toward an understanding with snow. As much as we sometimes want to deny it's presence, we cannot avoid the stuff. Snow sieves through window screens and drifts across the floorboards of the porch. It finds its way inside on our shoes, melts, and forms puddles on the kitchen floor. We look out the windows on sunny days, and while the brightness of the glow might support a fleeting thought of summer, a blinding whiteness asserts the truth.

Wet, floppy flakes start falling in autumn, sometimes as early as the last week of August. The first snow proves fugacious, here one morning, gone the next. But soon the stuff sticks. Then it stays stuck and piles up faster than junk mail. By the first of November, snow lies deep enough on the ground to spill into the open tops of shoes. By December, it's knee-deep. By January, walking beyond beaten paths is impossible without skis or snowshoes. A tall man sinks up to his private parts, and still his legs can't find the ground.

Children in our neck of the woods learn at an early age that every snowflake is unique. No two bear the same crystalline form, as examination under a microscope attests. Yet the individuality of snowflakes is hard for us adults who shovel snow, drive automobiles in snow, and pay better-equipped neighbors to plow our driveways free of snow to celebrate. After all, flakes appear by the million, and the dominion they achieve over the landscape and over our lives is achieved by overwhelming numbers.

Once snow settles for its siege, getting about in it becomes vital. Sanity, marriages, and friendships hang in the balance. As the fur trappers of earlier centuries knew, cabin fever comes from letting snow hold you prisoner, and it veers all too easily toward alcoholism, verbal ugliness, and violence. Debbie and I know this well. If we let winter keep us captive, we start to pick at each other. So at least once a week we get out—break out of confinement, thrash around in the white stuff for an hour or two, and let it be known publicly that we'll not let the occupying force push us around.

The most extreme example I know of the consequences of staying too long indoors in a northern winter, rather than confronting it head-on, involves seven American airmen in World War II. They were part of a squadron flying home to the

States from Europe in 1942 when a gale scattered the planes off Labrador. One of the pilots, a survivor of close encounters with the Luftwaffe, failed to reach the group's immediate destination, a base on the Canadian coast. The U.S. Army Air Corps presumed the plane and crew lost. No efforts were made at rescue.

Months later, Eskimos discovered a secret the military would not relinquish, at least in full, for fifty years. (Even then, it took a persistent assault by the crew's family members to wrest the full story from the Pentagon's secret-keepers.) The pilot had crash-landed the plane near the coast. No one on board suffered serious injury. What could the marooned men do? Their efforts to resuscitate the radio failed. Food and drink would last for a while, and aviation fuel could be burned to keep the cabin warm. So they huddled, conserving energy, and waited for rescue.

Weeks passed. As hopes grew faint, three of the party decided to make for the coast. They would inflate a raft, sail southward to a Canadian military base, and send help. But it never came. The men never reached the base. No trace of them has ever been found.

Meanwhile the Mississippi-born pilot and the remaining members of his crew, surrounded by snow too deep to cross on foot, made no effort to escape. A native village lay several miles away, but the men, who were fast losing their strength, put their faith in God and the U.S. Army. They might have fashioned snowshoes from tree limbs or from pieces of the aircraft. They might have tried to make their way out. But they did not. As the pilot's journal, found after it was too late, recorded, the men watched their rations dwindle, ran out of heating fuel, and spent their last days curled up together like puppies. One by one they died. They were doomed not by circumstance or bureaucratic indifference, at least not entirely, but in part by their own inability or unwillingness to travel over snow.

Heeding the lesson, I get out. Being a naturalist from a warmer clime, I find daily fascination in learning how the plants and animals of the Adirondacks cope with snow. Our nonhuman neighbors, like Debbie and me, must deal with the stuff one way or another.

Consider the most conspicuous organisms in our landscape, the trees. About half are deciduous, shedding their leaves around the time snow begins to linger. This is surely no accident of evolution. A rare early snowfall, which can be counted on to bring flakes that are wet and sticky, coats leaves thickly. Before long the weight of crystal exceeds the carrying capacity of limbs, and down they come, leaves, branches, empty birds' nests, and all. For this and other reasons, scientists believe, northern deciduous trees evolved the habit of beating the snow to the punch. In early October, they jettison their leaves in a blizzard of red and orange.

Our white world also includes evergreens. I write these words on the sixteenth of January and look out my office window to the south, where through a veil of falling snow I make out a colonnade of balsam firs. These tall, dark cousins of pines bear along their twigs needles that bristle like the tines of a hairbrush. When abused, the needles bend rather than break, a feature that helps them withstand assault by snow. And the shape of the tree itself, steeple-topped, more narrow than wide, with ranks of branches sweeping toward the ground, makes certain that gravity has no trouble grooming it of snow that might otherwise accumulate and pull the thing down.

Beneath the white that submerges landscape, not all plants lie dead or barren of leaves, despite their entombment. *Lycopodia,* or club-mosses, manage to stay upright and green, and so do the Christmas fern and mountain wood fern. If you scoop away the snow, you find these natives looking none the worse for burial. Photosynthesis ceases in the subnivean gloom, but as the snow grows thin in spring, light begins to penetrate. Leaf cells resume manufacturing sugar while those of deciduous neighbors are still folded in the bud.

Even for plants that surrender their leaves, snow provides benefits. A thick, consistent cover insulates the soil, protecting roots, bulbs, seeds, and symbiotic fungi against deep freezing. Two winters ago, in February, I marched outdoors with an iron pipe on which to mount a bird feeder and hammered it into the ground. I was certain the soil would be rock-hard. To my surprise, the pipe slid through ten feet of snow compressed to four, struck the dirt, and with the blows of my sledge, penetrated easily. Bare soil, by contrast, may freeze to a depth of four feet or more.

For wild animals, snow represents a mixed blessing. Creatures such as terrestrial insects that tend to spend the winter quiescent in the soil as eggs or pupae benefit from the stuff. Moles prosper, too, the more snow the better. Soft soil under snowpack agrees with their earthworm lifestyle far more than does naked dirt frozen to the consistency of granite. Shrews, which often travel in mole tunnels and feed upon their makers, flourish accordingly. Studies show the short-tailed shrew often gains weight in winter and may reach its greatest numbers.

A fine thing about snow, if you're a small mammal and can manage to get around beneath it, is that it affords a shield from the prying eyes and intrusive noses of predators. Hawks and owls have a hard time hunting in snow, except for those far northern species that specialize in it. Foxes and coyotes struggle, too, although they've learned to listen for movements beneath the snow, leap into the air, and pounce on the appropriate spots. Typically, the four-legged hunters catch, or try to catch, voles. Voles, close cousins to lemmings, are mouse-sized mammals with short tails, small ears, and bread-loaf-shaped bodies.

No human has any business projecting his sentiments on animals, but I can't helping thinking voles relish white winters. We find the evidence when the snow surrenders to the sun in May. Vole empires are revealed. They consist of beaten paths turning this way and that, broad avenues, important intersections, piles of cut grass suggesting stacks of firewood, and holes plunging where the human eye cannot follow. Occasionally I find a vole frozen quite literally in its tracks. I'm reminded of Pompei and Herculaneum, except that here, sunshine and warm spring days take the place of archeologists.

For animals that move above the snow, the Adirondack winter poses greater challenges. Red squirrels nearly avoid the ground altogether, commuting from tree to tree and descending only when cutting winds or unrequited appetites drive them into burrows stocked with nuts. But what of the snowshoe hare? This hirsute cousin of the cottontail rabbit weighs four pounds or more. It cannot climb. It doesn't burrow. Fortunately, evolution has equipped the hare with a solution. In autumn, its hind feet, prodigious even for a lagomorph, sprout an extravagant array of stiff hairs. These—

the eponymous snowshoes—splay out from the toes, enlarging their surface area. When powder lies deep on the ground, predators such as the red fox and bobcat find it hard going, but hares pad across the top. This morning I found hare tracks in a place where the snow lay six feet deep. The footprints, occurring in clusters of four, barely dimpled the surface.

Hares not only endure snow, they profit from it. As drifts pile higher, they become elevators, carrying animals to new and higher feeding places. Twigs, buds, and bark provide most of the winter diet, and snow helps the hares to find it.

My own snowshoes, built in a factory, consist of aircraft-grade aluminum and plastic webbing. When I venture afield on them, I find that the hares and I are not alone in our ability to transcend the powder. Tracks with four points, three facing forward and one backward, testify to the perambulations of grouse.

Ruffed grouse, cousins to the chicken and turkey, raise breast feathers when courting or frightened, suggesting Elizabethan collars and giving the birds the adjectival half of their name. In winter, bristles called pectinations develop between their toes. These allow a plump grouse (and all healthy grouse are plump) to float on snow rather than sink.

New snow serves as the world's best muffler of sound. On mornings after winter storms, I snowshoe through a silence so profound the quiet of the grave could not exceed it. Imagine my shock when, just ahead, the powder explodes with a spray and roar. For a moment, I'm flummoxed. Then I see: a grouse rockets for cover. The bird had burrowed in the snow to pass a cold night in comfort, and I've blundered on the bivouac. While it might seem perverse to spend a cold night immersed in ice crystals, there's method in the madness, as the grouse and the Inuit peoples of the Arctic know well. Beneath the snow, the temperature hovers around the freezing mark. Above, it plunges. Our coldest night this winter brought a thermometer reading of thirty-six degrees below zero Fahrenheit.

Of all the creatures that manage to flourish atop Adirondack snow, the most remarkable in terms of its abundance and size is the snow flea, *Hypogastrura tooliki*. On sunny days, especially in late winter, these animated decimal points pour out of the soil, migrate up the trunks of trees and shrubs, and spill over the snow in great black masses. Look closely and you see can see them move. The tails work like springs, tensing and releasing in propulsive whipcracks. Snow fleas are not true fleas of the order *Siphonoptera* but primitive insects called Collembolans. Some scientists believe they feed on algae and bits of organic material deposited on snow by gravity and wind, while others speculate that the masses we see eat nothing but simply erupt from burgeoning populations in the soil. We see the miniscule animals in great clusters, easily mistaken at a glance for shadows.

The most conspicuous animal in our winter landscape, a titan beside the snow flea, makes its presence known early in the season, then vanishes. The change comes with a heavy snowfall. One day our lawn is crisscrossed by virtual highways of hoof prints, and the next a new snow erases them. Weeks and months pass. We will not see the white-tailed deer and its tracks again until a long warm spell reduces the crystalline depths.

What happens? The white-tailed deer is a relatively short-legged, low-slung beast better adapted to the mild climates of the southern United States than to the Arctic conditions of the Adirondack winter. Handicapped by cloven, pointed feet that pierce even crusty snow, the deer gets bogged as the snow level rises. So whitetails migrate to quiet, sheltered places called "yards." There the snow is less deep, and the deer that share the yard keep it trampled. All is well, if the period of confinement is brief. But in long hard winters, the deer in a yard deplete its limited supply of twigs, buds, and bark. Starvation sets in, diseases flare, and coyotes and bobcats start picking off the weak.

For the moose, the whitetail's northern cousin, Adirondack snow generally provides only a minor inconvenience. This largest of the world's deer is perfectly designed for surviving our cold, snowy winters. Start with the torso: bigger than a bathtub, covered thickly with hair, possessing a low surface-area-to-volume ratio that helps it to retain heat. This prodigious mass of muscle, blood, and viscera travels on four legs so long and slender they would look at home, if shaved, in a chorus line. The hip and shoulder joints are formed in such a way that the moose can lift its legs nearly as high as its back—a handy trick in February. Now add the moose's head: a massive thing, mounted on the pinnacle of a tree-trunk neck, perfect for reaching high and biting off winter greens.

The moose is superbly adapted for life in snow, but snow still finds a way to bring the leviathans down. Studies of moose and gray wolves on Isle Royale in Lake Superior show that when a moose grows old, arthritis may hobble it. The once nimble beast labors through deep powder where it once would have danced, and wolves seize the opportunity.

Snow imposes physical demands, as we've seen, but there are psychological hurdles, too. Given the difficulty of conducting interviews with grouse, ungulates, and lagomorphs, I must rely on my own testimony to illustrate.

Last November, I decided to try my hand at hunting. For a great many men and an enthusiastic minority of women in our part of the world, hunting deer is an annual ritual that connects them to the great currents of life, and brings communion with ancestors who stalked venison on the hoof as a matter of survival. My uncle, who grew up in the Adirondacks, had given me a Winchester, sold to him secondhand in the 1940s. The thing, like the man who sold it, was an antique. But I was in luck. My uncle had kept the rifle in good working order, and our local sporting goods store sold ammunition that fit it. One morning I loaded the gun and set off into the woods on snowshoes.

Would I shoot a deer if I had the chance? I might, and I might not. The prospect of fresh meat appealed to me, but not the act of killing. If I were to catch a deer in my sights, squeeze the trigger, and make a competent shot, gutting, hauling, and butchering would be required, too. So off I went, eager, yet with reservations.

For about a half hour, I plodded through four or five feet of powder, following hoof prints. Hunting season comes early in the winter, before the deer have yarded. The tracks led right and left, up hills and down, circled back on themselves, and set off in new directions. After a while, I realized something unsettling. I had lost confidence that I knew the direction home.

What to do? I felt a jolt of fear. The sky—what little of it I could see amid the trees—had turned white and curdled with the approach of a front. Without the sun, I would need a compass to find my way home. Fortunately, I had brought one and knew how to use it.

The needle pointed me north, which meant that I had come from the right. I was astounded. The direction seemed all wrong—west rather than east.

Under most circumstances, my ability to orient is acute. My wife and I had wandered far into the same woods on a hot afternoon the previous July, and even though she, an excellent navigator of automobiles, had become disoriented and anxious, I was able to reckon the direction by sun angle and gut feeling and lead us without deviation to our door. But things were different in snow. The view in every direction appeared exactly the same—white above, white below, the forest a latticework of snow clinging to twigs, limbs, and trunks. Claustrophobia crept over me. Snow had wrapped itself tightly around every object in this landscape, and if I stood still long enough, I'd be encrusted by it, too.

I could have taken a clue from Daedelus and escaped by following the thread of my tracks. But I had walked a labyrinth to get where I had gotten and rebelled at the idea of facing the twists and turns anew. A direct route would bring me home swiftly. But where did it lie? My first thought was to put away the compass (surely a magnetized rock was deflecting the pointer), but a deeper, wiser instinct, one wired for survival, spoke from my brain stem. It said plainly: "When in doubt, trust the compass."

For a half hour or more, as the light of the forest dimmed, I struggled through powder so deep and loose it often swallowed up my snowshoes, sending me face-first, cursing, into the fluff. I pushed through drifts up to my waist. Thoughts of hunting were forgotten. Every watt of my energy, psychic and otherwise, was devoted to securing my deliverance. It wouldn't come easily. Fallen trees and leaning trunks broke my line of travel again and again, forcing me to detour through ever more snow.

My fear was not acute, but it nagged. Thoughts of Jack London's "To Build A Fire" drifted in and out of mind. In that tale the narrator, an inexperienced traveler on a lethally cold night in the Yukon, feels the snow give way beneath him. He breaks through a thin pane of ice covering a stream. Water soaks his clothes. He'll be dead in minutes if he can't ignite a fire. In a conventional story, the man would struggle, then prevail. In this one, he builds his blaze under a tree, and the warmth from it causes the snow on an overhanging branch to fall. The flames are extinguished and with them, by implication, the narrator's life. When the tale ends, we know the man has frozen to death.

If I got stuck out overnight, I would take a lesson from London and make a fire carefully. Dry matches rested safely in a pack on my back, and the woods were thick with fuel. For shelter, I would use a snowshoe as a shovel and with it heap up a big pile of snow. In a couple of hours, those unique crystals would interlock in a process called destructive metamorphism. Then I could safely dig out a cave in the middle, crawl inside, and stay as warm as a grouse until morning. Snow kills, and snow saves.

I stopped to rest. Soaking my clothes with perspiration would lead to hypothermia, and I felt myself growing damp. Where was home? Its appearance was overdue. I had a vision. Through the trees I saw a house, one I didn't recognize. How could this be? We have few neighbors, and I know their places well. It took longer than I care to admit to realize that I was viewing a neighbor's shingled house from an unfamiliar angle—an angle that meant I was standing within a few feet of the road on which we live.

The sensible thing would have been to admit the errors of my navigation, make the last few steps to civilization, and scuff home along the pavement. Instead, I plunged back into the woods. Circling in the direction in which I now knew home lay, I thrashed through powder, brush, and debris for another half hour. Again I emerged—in the same place!

I laughed, even though I wanted to curse the snow and the cold and the suffocating whiteness that turned the familiar woods of summer into an adversary. Again I marched into the labyrinth. This time I made it out, physically and mentally spent.

Making the last steps toward our house, I looked around and in the last clarion light of day, saw the snow afresh. There was no romance in it, nor any hostility. Like most things in the Universe, the snow was supremely indifferent to life. It simply *was*. After all, it's only water. Why does the mind delude itself otherwise? In a warm room, with a hot cup of tea in my belly, I could look out and project beauty on it if I wanted to—paint one of those scenes of snow-covered cottages and landscapes whose sharp angles and junk piles, abandoned automobiles and bulldozer ruts, have been erased by flowing drifts of white. Or, stranded overnight in the winter woods, lost, despondent, shivering in a snow cave, I could look out in the unpitying moonlight and see a cruel element bent on my annihilation. But these would be fictions. The truth about snow is that it exists, and we make of it what we will.

III. THE ADIRONDACK SEASONS

Spring

Today, I gaze out my office window and take in a scene hard to envision a week ago: the sight of a great arc of water, black as octopus ink, pouring past the north end of our driveway.

Spring is coming. The ice has gone out on the Saranac River.

Late last night, I took a walk to deliver a few papers. It was late. My wife and son lay in bed asleep. So were the neighbors in whose mudroom a quarter mile away I'd been asked to drop off the documents.

Out in the darkness I was not the only prowler on the move. As I neared the river, a large unseen object punched the glassy surface. Boom! Next came an enormous splash, as if a swimmer had cannonballed off a bridge.

I was startled but needn't have been. The disturber of the peace was well known to me. Soon I had a flashlight on a corpulent rodent with a pancake for a tail. Its eyes glowed yellow-green in the beam.

A beaver.

Sometimes light will provoke a beaver to slap its tail and plunge. We call one of the beavers that cruises our section of stream "Twitchy" because it dunks on the slightest provocation, not just once but again and again. We imagine one of the older beavers sitting Twitchy down and telling him or her that wise old folk-tale, "Never Cry Wolf."

Last night's beaver slapped only once. And rather than flee, it lingered, swimming this way and that as if it enjoyed my attentions. I doubt it did, yet there was something so relaxed, so devil-may-care about the animal's movements that I'm tempted to say it was happy.

Why only tempted? Scientists frown on anyone who credits a forty-pound rodent, or any other animal besides the one writing this sentence, with emotion. Feelings are hard to prove in animals that can't or won't comment on ink-blots. I've always suspected, however, that animals do experience emotion. If they do, what better occasion than ice-out after a long winter to induce cheerful sentiments in a beaver?

All through the months of ice, cold, and snow, the beaver and its fellow lodge members survive on canned goods. Well, not really canned goods, but in late summer and autumn they cut up great masses of twigs and limbs and stash them in the muddy bottom. There they can get at the stuff under the ice, exiting the lodge via an underwater portal, swimming to the pantry, and hauling back meals in their teeth.

Then come days of low, grinding sounds. Suddenly the roof of ice, which has covered the river all through the long Adirondack winter, breaks up into school-bus-sized slabs. It's like an old-fashioned log drive as the slabs smash into each other and pile up in backwaters. For the beavers, the world is flooded with light.

This is the best time of year for beaver-watching. Suddenly the big rodents are everywhere, day and night, pushing impressive bow waves ahead of them as they ply the river's surface like barges. They're out of the water, too, trudging up banks to preen wet fur and gnaw the trunks of trees with their formidable pumpkin-colored incisors.

I concede the possibility that beavers live lives bereft of emotion, that they shift from winter habits into spring on autopilot, unthinking, unfeeling, just doing their jobs. But things I see make me wonder. After ice-out, beavers spend a good deal of time simply basking in the sunshine, and it looks to me like they savor every moment.

Tonight, behind in my work, I burn the midnight oil, staying up past one in the morning. I finally call it quits at 1:30 a.m. Staggering back to the house for bed, I soak up a little of the peace of the night until it strikes me that the night is anything but peaceful.

The night screams with action. In the woods behind the house, I hear the throaty, energetic hooting of a barred owl. The bird is hard at work, hunting rodents, courting its mate, letting rivals know that its territory will be defended. Only dawn will send the owl to its rest.

In another direction, toward the river, I hear the shrill voices of amphibians. Toads blare drawn-out trills, the notes going on and on for ten seconds or more until puffy throats are drained of wind. One toad's torch song overlaps another's and another's, so that they pile up like a multitrack recording. The impressive result is a towering wedding cake of sound.

And there's more. For every toad that sings, and there are dozens, a hundred monosyllabic spring peepers plead, *Me, me!* to every female that will listen. In the aggregate, peeper voices form a sky-high curtain of sound, one that, when I close my eyes and let my mind drift, reminds me of winter sleigh bells.

Out here in the dark, I can't see any wildlife, but I hear plenty and know that my ears take in a mere fraction of an enormous and vibrant whole. Foxes prowl, bobcats ambush, coyotes stalk, weasels chase, mice gnaw, worms mate, pollen pollinates, fish swim, bats blare out sonar, and way up in the sky, songbirds migrate. The more I think about it, the clearer it becomes that the night throbs with action.

Life may or may not have evolved on Mars, but there's no question it permeates every dimension of our beloved planet Earth. From Antarctica to the Arctic and from boiling submarine trenches in the mid-Atlantic to the icy summits of the world's tallest mountains, organisms and microorganisms flourish in staggering abundance. Yet life hasn't confined its conquests to geography. It shows equal adaptability in colonizing every one of the twenty-four hours.

No matter the hour when I open my eyes and ears these days, I find life burgeoning all around me. At 4:30 in the morning, as the day's first light seeps into the forest, songbirds are already up and warbling. At dusk, a male woodcock struts in our meadow, alternating nasal ground calls with high-altitude caroling and acrobatics. At midday, the blue sky fills with puffy clouds, clouds largely inflated with moisture sucked from moist earth by trees, then exhaled through pores in the leaves.

Is there a time when life takes a rest? I can't think of any. The action, especially at this time of year, is relentless. From the melancholy whistle of a white-throated sparrow at 3 a.m. until the chatter of a red squirrel twelve hours later, and then around again, life and the hour-hands on the clock cartwheel together, breathing, feeding, birthing, and dying incessantly, as they will until an unthinkable day billions of years hence when our dying sun swallows up the Earth and all its life is incinerated. Even then, electrons will continue to race around protons. Our chemical constituents will rise again somewhere in another time, another place or galaxy.

The mind boggles to think in universal terms, especially when the body is weary. I turn away from the stars, head for a soft pillow, and leave the night to my neighbors.

After a long, cold winter, spring in the northern Adirondacks arrives not in a single flourish but as a striptease. The sun climbs higher in the sky. Breezes warm. Snow banks retreat. But wait. Just when you think you're going to see the landscape fully bared, cold returns, halting the show, or worse, a late snowfall commits an act of censorship, taking your first peek at spring and wrapping it beneath new layers of concealment.

Spring's arrival stirs my blood. It's playful, roundabout, tantalizing. One moment I'm walking along shivering, the next I wade into a pocket of warm air. In the warm, I smell spring as well as feel it. There's a heady fragrance in the air, one part old life decaying, one part new life being born.

Birds are coy. One day I'm out in the yard and all, in terms of ornithology, is wintry. Only the chickadees, woodpeckers, and nuthatches of January and February flit around the feeder. If the sun is bright, chickadees may sing *Dee-dee* and woodpeckers drum on hollow trunks. These sounds constitute breeding behavior, yet I hear them on mild days in January, too.

Then come surprises. I walk out the back door and, although the landscape looks no different than it did the day before, something seems different. A few seconds pass before I figure it out. Of course! Brown creepers belt out high, tinkling notes that leave a sonic sparkle in the air everywhere I turn.

The brown creeper is a drab, warbler-sized bird with a thin bill that curves downward. It's the kind of animal you don't pay much attention to until you learn its song. Creepers are more often heard than seen, which is perhaps as it should be. For me, their bursts of song in March represent the first convincing proof of spring.

Blackbirds also bring glad tidings. They turned up in our neighborhood a few days ago, filling selected treetops with raucous cackling and squeaking. Scrutinize a flock with a pair of field glasses, and you'll usually find that it contains birds of more than one species. The spring flocks I see in the Adirondacks typically contain redwings and common grackles. Sometimes amid them I spy rusty blackbirds, which look like hybrids of the other two.

Canada geese proclaim spring's onset, too, yet like most signs of the season, they can't be trusted. One day I look up to the sound of honking and spy a wedge of 100 or more geese flapping northward. I want to rejoice, but I know that the next day the weather may turn cold and I'll watch the same birds retreating southward.

Wildflowers? I have yet to see any. The first I spy are usually overlooked by most people: the tiny lurid-pink female blossoms of a common Adirondack shrub called beaked hazelnut. It requires a microscope or strong hand lens to fully appreciate these tiny flowers, but their electric color makes the effort worth all the trouble.

I find it hard to pick favorites, but among the early portends of spring in my part of the world I probably most savor the return of fragrances to my nostrils and the pink wash that spreads over hillsides at the end of March. Winter is the season of no smells. For the olfactory lobe, it's a barren time of year. Then, the first thaw summons odors from sodden soils. I'm never sure what I'm smelling, but it doesn't matter. The nose rejoices. Hillsides blush as red maple buds swell in preparation for flowering. Day by day, the pink grows stronger, until one warm, sunny morning the blossoms start bursting open like popcorn.

Red maples are like people in that some are males and others are females. The male flowers combine yellow filaments with red anthers, creating an impression at a distance of orange. The female flowers are entirely red. So you can drive down a highway on an early spring day, noting a boy maple here and a girl there. When this happens, there's no turning back. The season has revealed itself at last.

Hang on! April takes aim for May, and spring's bucking bronco ride across the Adirondacks has begun. The sun grows strong, snow melts, the ground turns to mud, brooks roar, migrating birds pour from the sky, fish spawn, woodchucks burst from their hibernacula, chipmunks reappear, insect populations explode, and much, much more. Don't blink! In a headlong rush that overwhelms the mind and senses, we charge from winter to summer as staggering developments occur minute by thrilling minute.

Spring's transformation of the landscapes of the Adirondacks forever astounds me. Living in the midst of it is like witnessing the evolution of life on Earth. In the beginning is barren rock and lifeless ground. Then come warm rains and the alchemy of photosynthesis and sunshine, spurring the growth of algae, wildflowers, and fungi. Trees that looked moribund all winter suddenly come to life, their buds spewing new leaves, blossoms, and pollen.

Meanwhile in the animal kingdom, tiny copepods barely visible to the naked eye stir in meltwater ponds. Insects spangle the air, and our distant cousins the amphibians, the croaking frogs and the stoical salamanders, rise out of the ancestral muck to feed on their invertebrate brethren and reproduce.

Watch closely now. Reptiles begin to appear, one here, one there. Where I live, I see mainly garter snakes, painted turtles, and snapping turtles. As the sun cooks the land, reptiles rise, shine, and proliferate.

Meanwhile, overhead, the sky fills with birds. Early arrivals, appearing hard on the heels of the snowmelt, include the robin, the bluebird, the red-winged blackbird, and the woodcock. Song sparrows appear early, too, and their chiming voices announce winter's demise.

Who's that? A phoebe, just arrived from Guadalajara. There? A turkey vulture, cruising for corpses. That soft trill broadcast from the maple? It's the voice of the myrtle or yellow-rumped warbler. In the swamp? The staccato carol of the northern waterthrush. So swiftly do birds multiply and diversify that even the expert birdwatcher has a hard time keeping up.

Then there's our mob, the mammals. No sooner does the earth soften than moles are pushing it up, decorating the turf with ridges that look like miniature versions of the serpentine mounds Indians built centuries ago in the Ohio Valley. White-tailed deer shed guard hairs in clumps, which you find on the ground during the weeks they're turning themselves from gray to cinnamon. Chipmunks rocket out of winter lairs to show their stripes, and the ponderous woodchuck settles Buddha-like into it's hot-weather job of putting on fat.

Bats return to the sky. Some have hibernated, others migrated. Raccoons crawl out of the tree hollows in which they've snoozed away the winter, and skunks lumber out of burrows and crevices. In my estimation, one of the great sights of spring in our part of the world is seeing a mother skunk crossing a patch of green grass, her tail held high, while a half dozen or so skunklets trail in single file behind her.

I wish I could slow down spring, stretch its rush of wonders out over a broader expanse of time. When a blackpoll warbler flies through on its way to the Far North, I want to freeze it in place and savor its presence. But that's not the way spring works. All any of us can do is stand amidst the torrent, swim if we dare, and savor all the details we can gather into consciousness. Soon enough, the show will be over, and the wait until the next performance is long.

Debbie and I are about to turn out the last light in the house when we hear a sound. It's a small knock, coming from the direction of the kitchen.

A mouse? That's my theory until the noise comes again, slightly louder this time. Curiosity aroused, the two of us head for the kitchen.

Nothing appears amiss. But the sound comes again, even louder. We realize it originates not inside, but outside the back door. Something or someone has tipped over a metal garbage can filled with birdseed and is raiding the contents.

A raccoon? A bear? A neighbor with an inordinate fondness for sunflower seed? Despite our eagerness to solve the crime, we hesitate to open the door to the mudroom, where an outside light switch is located. To do so will mean unlocking the kitchen door, which is secured by a deadbolt. This will leave only a flimsy storm door between our pajama-clad tenderloins and a big carnivore, if in fact the thief is a bear.

So we fetch a flashlight and aim toward the source of the commotion. Egad! The light illuminates not the average modestly proportioned black bear, but a particularly large one. We've seen enough bears over the years to have a sense of relative size, and this animal is on the substantial side.

How much does it weigh? There's no way to say, and I'm not about to hand it the bathroom scale. Record weights for male black bears range up to about 900 pounds. We guess conservatively. Our oversized bruin, not long out of its hibernaculum, probably weighs a mere four or five hundred.

Still, that many pounds of fleet-footed, strong-muscled, toothy carnivore, so close at hand, gives us pause. In fact, even the paws give us pause. They're the size of ping-pong paddles but hairier. From them stout claws arch, the perfect tools for climbing trees, tearing open yellow jacket nests, and raking up wild blueberries and bird seed.

We watch for a few thrilling and unnerving minutes. From time to time, the bear extracts its head from the trash can and looks us squarely in the eye. Its retinas glow a bright yellow, like dog eyes in the headlights of a car. The muzzle, tinged with brown, is far too big to circle with two hands, or at least that's how I size it up at a distance.

What now? We could watch the bear all night, but a nettlesome thought intrudes on our enjoyment of the performance. What if he, or she, sniffs food in the kitchen and decides to come inside for dessert? Bears have been known to do such things. A glance affirms that our insubstantial storm and inner doors would slow it down only a little.

So we do what the experts advise. We make a lot of noise. Our shouts drive the bear away, but only about thirty feet. There it noses the remains of three bird feeders it demolished before discovering the trash can. Finding nothing, it turns and lopes back toward the kitchen door.

Watching the bear approach, we have our best look yet at its glossy, ebony bulk. This beast is massive. Its legs are long and arm-like, and the easy confidence with which it moves on them suggests superhuman power and speed. I wouldn't want to challenge this animal to a brawl or foot-race.

The bear plunges its face back into the garbage can, and we decide it's high time to drive it off. Debbie grabs a saucepan and metal spoon, and I cup my hands. While she clangs, I clap in such a way as to make sounds like gunshots. The bear yanks out its head, pirouettes, and bounds into the woods.

Will we sleep well tonight? You can guess the answer.

Thank the universe or heaven for springtime and new leaves. In early May, or thereabouts, the weary post-winter Adirondack landscape of grays and browns suddenly comes green again. For the miracle we must thank chlorophyll, a magnesium-based pigment not unlike the iron-fortified hemoglobin in our bloodstreams. Invented a couple of billion years ago by marine cyanobacteria, improved and put to good use by seaweeds, and eventually carried on land by plants, chlorophyll turns the organisms who possess it into alchemists, ones able to conjure biological energy out of golden sunshine.

It's a neat trick. Although I studied the details in college, I've forgotten them save for elegant turns of phrase such as "oxidative phosphorylation" and the "Krebs cycle." Still, one doesn't need to know the fine points of photosynthesis to savor the phenomenon itself. Just sit back in a rocking chair and watch the world turn green.

From where I sit, I look out three tall windows into the limbs and twigs of a wild black cherry tree. It's not much of a tree, crooked and scabby in places with a sort of fungal eczema, but hour by hour the cherry unfurls its complement of leaves. They're thin and pointed as they emerge and colored a drab olive green. But green is green after a long winter, and I'm glad to see them.

I also look out at quaking aspens, or "popples," as my neighbors call them. Their leaves are farther along than those of the cherry, each one a flag twice the size of a postage stamp and as soft and tender as the skin of a newborn baby. Upon opening, quaking aspen leaves are colored the same luminous green as limes.

Evergreen trees also meet my gaze—white pines, balsam firs, and red spruces. Sure, they've been green all winter, but with warm weather and sunshine triggering the manufacture of fresh chlorophyll, they're looking their best. Soon the dark green balsam twigs will sport new growth in the form of pale green tips. It's as if the sedate trees of Christmas have decided to celebrate the coming summer by having a hairdresser give them highlights.

Spring

Yesterday I came upon foliage so buoyantly green that I nearly gasped when I saw it. I was scouting a trail for clients of my Adirondack guiding business when I happened to look down at the right moment. There, at the base of a tree in a spot I'd overlooked while passing it the first time, trembled the delicate, many-fingered leaves of a wildflower called wood anemone.

The plants were blooming, and the pink-white flowers were pretty. But it was the leaves that tugged at my consciousness, leaves so lush despite their miniature size that they could not be ignored. Soon maple, beech, and birch foliage will shade the wood anemone, and it will shrivel in response. But for the moment, the little plant makes flowers and fruit while the sun shines, and its chlorophyll-colored leaves are the finest in the woods.

Every once in a while, circumstances conspire to bring the birds of a broad area together into a small space. It might be a late, deep snowfall that lures every worm-starved American robin to the same lightly dusted meadow. Or it could be a tropical storm that forces thousands of migrants to fall like hailstones on a back yard or city park.

Today it's the temperature. Insect-eating birds from faraway southern lands are with us now, but the weather isn't welcoming. Hard freezes at night and cold, windy days are depressing the bugs. If the birds can't find emergency rations, they're goners.

Early this morning, a friend gave me a tip. Visit the brushy south shore of Moody Pond in Saranac Lake, he said, and you'll see more birds in ten minutes than you've seen all spring. What's up? Mayflies are surging by the thousands to the water's surface, and the north wind is plowing them toward the pond's southern shore. The birds have discovered this, and warblers normally found high in trees or deep in thickets are out in the open, capitalizing on the bonanza.

It sounds too good to be true and almost is. When I arrive at the pond, a street-sweeping machine has roared through, scouring the road of sand and scattering the birds to the four points of the compass.

Yet the birds are not so easily put off. They come flitting back, one here, two there, some of them singing, others not. Within a minute or two, I'm seeing more warblers than I can count.

The only ones not picking over the shore are black-and-white warblers. The little specialists are doing what they always do: looking like crosses between songbirds and zebras, and gleaning insects and insect eggs from tree trunks.

I see blackpoll warblers, too. Like the black-and-white warblers they vaguely resemble, the blackpolls are singing as well as feeding. The black-and-white's song is a thin *zeedle, zeedle, zeedle.* The blackpoll broadcasts a string of notes all on the same pitch, the volume rising to a crescendo in the middle, then diminishing. Blackpoll warblers have black "polls" or caps and look vaguely like chickadees.

I'm used to looking up at the bellies of blackpoll warblers as they feed or sing way up in the treetops, but these birds flit just beyond arm's reach in low shrubs or hop along the ground. I look down on them, noting features I've never seen before this: greenish flight feathers and wing coverts and vibrant yellow-orange legs.

A Blackburnian warbler flits into view. Not one, but two, three, then four. This is another upper-story species that I'm not used to seeing low down and close at hand. Every one

I spy is a male, and it's dazzling. The Blackburnian is the monarch butterfly among our warblers. Black streaks contrast dramatically with a flaming orange head and neck.

I hear a familiar song with a flourish at the end. Is it the voice of a magnolia warbler or an American redstart? I soon see both birds, but it's the orange-and-black redstart that's singing.

Myrtle or yellow-rumped warblers are everywhere, and so, I discover, are black-throated blue warblers. Males and female black-throated blues appear in about equal number, the males calling attention to themselves with soft, dreamy trills. The male black-throated blue has a blue back, white belly, and ebony throat and flanks. The camouflaged female is a drab olive-green.

The birds I'm most excited to find appear last: two bay-breasted warblers, a single Canada warbler, and several Cape Mays. To describe these birds is to deny them aesthetic justice. No words, painting, or photograph can convey the pleasure of seeing them in the wild. Their patterns and colors combine in ways that, for sheer beauty, exceed the sum of their parts.

Some ventures in search of birds turn into nightmares. This one proves a dream—a lovely dream shot through with color and stereophonic sound. I hate for it to end, but responsibilities press. I leave the birds to their work, as I turn homeward to mine.

A dog's bark pierces the clamor of a froggy spring night. Sleeping on a screened porch, Debbie and I are roused from sleep. The cry repeats. I look at the clock. It's 2 a.m. Another bark. The voice sounds no more like the woof of a domestic dog than the average karaoke performer sounds like Paul McCartney.

Who's speaking? There are no pet dogs nearby, and this doesn't sound like a stray. Coyotes? They prowl hereabouts, but we're familiar with their yipping and wailing. Red fox or gray fox? These are our candidates. We've seen both in the yard, blinking up in the car headlights or streaking across the lawn in moonlight.

Lifelong students of nature, Debbie and I find it hard to leave a stone unturned (there might be a snake or salamander under it) or an animal's voice unidentified. We live in a perpetual state of discovery, looking, listening, posing questions, then rummaging in books, journals, recordings, and memory for the answers we can't glean in the field.

This time we do our homework but remain stumped. Fox vocalizations are described vaguely. It seems the experts remain as much in the dark as we are.

When the mystery animal barks on subsequent nights, its dry utterances echoing between our house and a wall of trees, we scour the darkness with a high-powered flashlight. Of fox, red or gray, there is no sign.

One morning I make a thorough search of the sound's apparent point of origin, the place where a one-lane bridge crosses the Saranac River. It's a perfect singing post, with open broadcasting range in all directions. I find nothing, not an animal, not a dropping, not a track in the sand.

Two years earlier, we'd heard similar sounds at night. Desperate for enlightenment, I'd contacted a friend who curates the world's largest library of natural sounds. Did he have red and gray fox recordings for us to listen to and compare? He did not. In fact, he appealed to me to keep up our vigil, make a tape, identify the barker, and then donate the recording to his collection.

But the case of the unseen vocalist remained open then, and it remains open still.

One day, perhaps, we will hear the voice again, charge into the night, and shine a light on the animal that opens its maw to make it. There will be an accompanying feeling of triumph, but also a countercurrent of disappointment—a letdown familiar to readers of Agatha Christie and Arthur Conan Doyle. Just as pleasures arise from gaining knowledge, so too they flow from being denied it.

I'm glad to know the songs of nearly every bird I hear and would not relinquish the hard-won knowledge for any price. Yet my gains come with a countervailing loss. Some of the mystery I once felt on spring mornings, when the air shook with a hundred voices I couldn't name, is gone. When I go camping and a weird sound rises in the darkness, I almost always know it for the call of a barred owl, or for the nuptial bleat of a frog whose scientific name I know by heart.

The next time the fox—or whatever it is—barks, I'll savor the mystery of its identity, even as I slip outside to shine a light on my ignorance.

I wake up in a black mood. Making a pot of coffee doesn't help to shake it. Dark feelings continue to ride heavily on my shoulders even after I step outside into a gorgeous spring morning. The sky is a brilliant blue, the sun bright and warming, and the morning air deliciously cool, yet all I can think of are past failings and future worries and the self-defeating bent of my thinking.

With work to do but no desire to do it, I wander into the woods, lured by a bird song. It's familiar yet unfamiliar, a voice I know well but haven't heard since last summer.

Picking my way among fallen trees, half interested in the bird's identity and half not giving a damn about anything, I advance a hundred feet. When trunks and limbs block further progress, I do something impulsive. I sit and wait.

Luck comes almost instantly. A tiny bird darts in and peers at me from behind a screen of young birch leaves. It's a male chestnut-sided warbler, a bird that looks fairly ordinary in a field guide but, perched two or three feet from the tip of my nose, dazzles me with its colors. The warbler wears a crown of gold, and bold streaks of chestnut run down its flanks, separating patterned green wings from a cream-white belly.

The warbler finds me puzzling. It flits from branch to branch, edging closer, until I feel like I can reach out a hand and touch it. As a museum visitor might circle a large sculpture, the warbler sizes me up from one angle, then another and another.

Self-consciousness returns with a start. Incredible! I suddenly realize I've left my head full of troubles behind. In sharing a moment of wonder with a bird, I've allowed my ego, with its ills, to take its rightful place as one small speck in a universe swarming with marvels.

As the day goes on, my funk never returns. I mull over the change. Why did a routine meeting with a bird I've seen hundreds of times produce such a lift? Did the incident trigger a pleasant association from the past, or simply give me something other than my own concerns to think about?

There was more to it, I think. By sitting quietly for a moment, ending my pursuit of the unknown singer and simply accepting whatever came my way, I came face to face with a reassuring truth. I am one of countless actors on a stage, not the star of a production. The chestnut-sided warbler was there, I was there, at least a dozen other birds caroled in the distance, bugs buzzed, flowers scented the air, and red squirrels chattered. Life surrounded me. So did death. Fallen leaves and toppled tree-trunks lay decaying everywhere I looked. It all seemed right and good.

We humans have a tendency to dominate nature, to oppose it, to separate ourselves from it, to fancy ourselves the very pearls of existence. In all these ways, we isolate ourselves from our fellow travelers on the planet. It's lonely being top dog. Yet we are not alone and certainly not top dog. We are part of Earth's great scheme of birth and growth and death and decay and birth again. Sometimes when we're feeling alienated, it feels best just to sit still, somewhere outdoors, and be reminded.

Twenty minutes before the alarm will blare, twenty minutes, that is, before 5 o'clock, I snap awake and can't fall back asleep. I'd love a few more winks but don't get them. At 4:50, I hear the coffee machine start to gurgle. At 4:55, I smell the coffee and lurch to my feet.

At 5:19, I'm standing outside on a chilly spring morning in the Adirondacks. The first bird I hear is a white-throated sparrow, whistling a plaintive *Old Old Sam Peabody-Peabody-Peabody*. Soon follows a fusillade of notes from the throat of a winter wren. Morning has been officially inaugurated although the sun has yet to rise.

Light precedes sunrise, of course, and it's filling the woods with a pale blue glow. I tread as quietly as I can (which is to say, not quietly at all) to a portable blind I set up a few days ago, a hundred yards west of our house. Inside the blind, deep in the woods, I'll sit, peer through a camera and lens, and if all goes well, make photographs of a ruffed grouse standing on a moss-covered log, beating the air with its wings.

Damn! I'm not early enough. The grouse is already at his post, and as I crunch toward the blind, he flies off. Not to be deterred, I haul my gear inside and prepare to be ready when the bird comes back. Perhaps it's an evil omen that as I slip inside the shelter, I notice a grouse perched in a tree overhead, watching me with suspicion.

By 5:45 I've drained a cup of coffee from my thermos, the woods have brightened, and the world seems well on its way to waking. A yellow-bellied sapsucker drums on a hollow tree, the last beats of its tattoo coming slowly and erratically. A chickadee whistles is territorial call, and both nuthatches sound off. The white-breasted nuthatch *yank-yank-yanks* at a measured tempo while the red-breasted nuthatch *ank-ank-ank-anks* as if it's in a hurry and has a train of insect larva to catch. I also hear the voices of an eastern phoebe, an American robin, and a red squirrel.

Suddenly I make out a distant but unmistakable sound that's familiar, yet I can't name its source. Wait—it's a wild turkey, a Tom, drunk on testosterone, gobbling like there's no tomorrow. It's the first such gobbling I've heard here.

A grouse drums nearby. Can it be mine? I peer out of a slit in the blind. No such luck. He's likely my bird, all right, but he's found another log.

A crow caws five times. A sapsucker screams *Bleer! Bleer! Bleer!* Now a grouse drums again. This one sounds like it's broadcasting from the warm bed I left behind. If I wasn't in an understanding mood, I'd curse it.

I'm frustrated. If I were to leave the blind and charge off in pursuit of the grouse's new auditorium, I'd scare it off along with every other bird in the woods. All I can do is wait and be hopeful.

At 6:03, I hear the warning beeper of a truck moving backwards on the road that passes our house. At 6:04, I hear the day's first blue jay. At 6:25, a dog barks. At 6:32, I hear a siren. A state trooper has pulled over the day's first speeder. At 6:39, I'm forced to concede that my toes are near-frozen and I'm shivering. At 6:42, I erupt with the first in a series of sneezes. At 6:58, the day's first purple finch warbles in my ears.

When a crow sounds the hour at 7:00, I decide to give up the morning's mission and go home. Sit in a living room and watch wildlife films on TV, and you may have little idea of the long hours and failed attempts that go into producing a modest snippet of footage. Yet I wouldn't trade ninety minutes in an easy chair for ninety minutes in the cold, cramped discomfort of the blind. Out here, the experience is so rich, the sensations so vivid, that even when I go home empty-handed I count the morning a success.

Every morning when I step outside to gulp the day's first mouthful of fresh air, I hear voices. Most sound as familiar to me as the speech of old friends or family members. Yet I haven't heard them in the Adirondacks for nearly a year.

Who's there? Yesterday a voice came from the top of a tree. It buzzed swiftly up a microtonal scale, then dropped abruptly at the end.

Hooray! Here caroled the year's first parula warbler, or at least, the first one in our yard. Handsomely painted in blue and yellow but favoring life in the treetops, this bird is hard to get a look at. But you can hear parula warblers easily and almost everywhere throughout these shaggy mountains.

A large part of the pleasure of identifying birds by sound, rather than sight, is remembering the hard work of learning the songs in the first place. There's a certain amount of suffering required to imprint a voice in your brain. Afterward, you're forever tickled with yourself that you persevered long enough—despite biting insects, thorns, poison ivy, and whatever else slowed you down—to transmute ignorance into savvy.

A week ago, I strolled down a neighbor's driveway with the morning's first cup of coffee in my hand and heard a sweet voice rising from the woods on my right. My brow wrinkled, then relaxed. Of course! This was a blue-headed vireo, back from its wintering haunts in the Deep South or Central America. Over and over it sang rising and falling two or three-note phrases, with long pauses between them.

How on Earth to pick a vireo out of the morning choir? A ranger named Anne Bellamy taught me the trick on a bird walk at Big Bend National Park in Texas. The year was 1982, and we were listening to a Bell's vireo, a western species. Bellamy called it "the question-and-answer bird," a name that applies equally well to most of our eastern species. According to Bellamy, the birds seem to say, *Who am I? Vireo. Who are you? I don't know.* The repetitive nature of the song and the way its phrases alternate with deliberate pauses give a vireo away.

One morning last week, Debbie and I stepped out to greet the day only to be saluted in return by a black-and-white warbler. It squeaked appealingly from the backside of a tree trunk. The song of this bird resembles the sound a gerbil makes when running on a metal wheel. Alerted to the bird's presence, we scanned the trees and soon saw a bird in black-and-white pinstripes darting further into the woods.

Chip-chip-chip-chap-chap-chap-chup-chup-chup. This burst of notes came from a thicket beside the river. It was a voice I hadn't heard since last July. I contemplated the setting and the sounds. Of course—a northern waterthrush, which is a kind of warbler, was announcing to its fellows and prospective mates that the long tropical vacation was over. May means breeding time for a waterthrush, with child-care duties to follow.

Who will it be tomorrow? It's not yet dinnertime, but already this late sleeper is looking forward to the next morning announcement, when a night-flying migrant opens its throat and broadcasts to all who listen, *Look at me! I'm here! Look what I can do!*

The now famous long, dog-legging putt that helped Tiger Woods win a Masters golf tournament was nothing compared to the hole in one recorded by Debbie, Ned, and me a few days ago. Admittedly, I'm biased. I have no more interest in whacking and chasing goiter-sized pock-faced balls around a manicured golf course all day than Tiger Woods probably has in crashing around woods and wetlands looking for birds. But if the feat performed by Woods represents his sport at its finest, then we have duplicated his triumph.

We found our own hole in one: the nest of a black-backed woodpecker.

Mind you, the black-backed is not just any old woodpecker. It is a boreal bird, a creature of the far North, which breeds in only a few cold, balsam-scented corners of the eastern United States.

One of those corners, it so happens, is our 18.5-acre ("more or less," as deeds up here say) property in the Adirondacks.

We've had occasional sightings of black-backed wood-peckers, often spaced a year or more apart. They've been tantalizing. The woodpeckers appear and linger for a few hours. They're big, they're tolerant of people gawking at them, and they seem very much at home. Take a walk, come back an hour later, and they're still chiseling at the same tree. But the next day, and the day after that, and for weeks and months afterward, the birds are either absent or invisible.

I don't know about Tiger's masterstroke, but our discovery of the black-backed nest involves a team effort. Ned gets the whole thing started. He insists we go for a walk.

Is our nature-loving toddler mindful of the 199 species on his life list of birds, and the fact that a black-backed woodpecker will bring him to 200? Perhaps not. Still, without Ned's push, we would have stayed at home.

Once we're moving, it's his parents' idea to cross the bridge that carries our road over the Saranac River. Ned dismisses the plan. Laughing, he takes off down a dirt track leading to a neighbor's hunting camp. Debbie and I grumble but follow.

Just north of the camp, beside a quiet oxbow of the river, the track circles back on itself. There Debbie makes her own pivotal contribution. "A black-backed woodpecker," she whispers. "Ned's 200th bird."

There it is—robust, black of back, hanging vertically near the top of a dead balsam fir. Debbie says it's a male. I can't agree until the bird flaps away, giving me a glimpse of the gold Debbie spied on top of the woodpecker's head.

What's that? I hear a pecking sound coming from the tree. A second woodpecker? None can be seen. So I circle around to the other side. In the process, I give our route a culminating dogleg, just like Tiger's famous putt.

One moment I'm peering at a plain brown trunk. The next a female black-backed woodpecker bursts from it like the puppet inside Ned's jack-in-the-box. As she rockets out to chase the male, I examine her point of origin with binoculars.

Aha! I find a round hole, seven feet above the mossy ground. Its diameter measures about two inches, and on the bottom, the wood just inside has been beveled neatly.

After we've all had a look, we back off. Unlike Tiger, who shared his triumph with the world, we'll keep ours a secret— it's location, anyhow. The birds will have a family to raise, and too many curious visitors might scare them off.

Still, I'll steal back for a peek now and again, staying far from the nest tree so my scent doesn't lead raccoons or weasels to the miracle unfolding inside.

Summer

Spring in the Adirondacks is over in a flash. One day the grass is greening, leaves unfold, and trees resound with birds newly arrived from the tropics. The next the lawn needs mowing, trees sport their hot-weather clothes, far northern breeders have vanished and taken their sweet songs with them, and we are left with the familiar birds of summer.

TeaCHER, teaCHER, teaCHER, TEACHER! That's an ovenbird staking out territory in the woods. *Cheery-up, cheerily, cheery-up, cheerily.* That's a robin lording over a domain rich in earthworms. A complex song suggestive of Beethoven rises symphonically from a thicket. That's a song sparrow telling its neighbors who's boss of the bushes.

It's time to start watching for nesting behavior. This morning, I watch a robin fly in and out of a hydrangea bush near our porch. I can tell the bird is a female because her colors appear faded, the breast a faint rusty orange, the head and back gray rather than the black.

What is the robin carrying? It bears something substantial in its mouth. A peek through the window screen reveals that the cargo is a mixture of mud and grass. With this home-grown adobe the bird constructs a nest that will endure for years but be used just once.

Around noon, I see the robin return to the hydrangea, settle onto the sturdy cup she's created, and do a sort of sitting-down dance. What is she up to? She vibrates her tail up and down and flutters her dusky wings.

I watch the bird perform the motions several times. Between acts she pivots slightly, changing her orientation. Before I continue I'll step outside, peek, and return here to report what, if anything, I find.

Here's the news. The nest is empty. Where I expected to find an egg, freshly laid and colored robin's egg blue (what else?), I see only wet, glistening mud. No wonder the female robin's belly looks dark these days. She's plopping mud in the nest, then using her bottom as a trowel.

Meanwhile tree swallows flutter around a birdhouse I mounted on a telephone pole, and blue jays with their own nests to tend suddenly grow silent. A female hummingbird visits a nectar feeder outside our kitchen window every few minutes. So swollen is her belly with eggs she can hardly bend over to sip.

The calendar says it's spring, but for the birds summer is underway. Long, busy days are the rule. Ornithologists speculate that certain adventurous tropical birds developed the habit of migrating toward the poles at least in part because the journey allows them to exploit a resource easily overlooked: the long buggy days of summer.

Far longer than the twelve-hour days that prevail year-round between the tropics of Cancer and Capricorn, the nearly eighteen hour days of early summer in the Adirondacks allow day-active animals more time for gathering foodstuffs. Might our own species have fled its equatorial cradle for similar reasons? I find pleasure in the notion.

* * *

Attention, please! When all is quiet in this Adirondack concert hall, the distinguished soloist makes his way to the stage. He walks purposefully, his body erect. With a deft bound, he leaps up to the platform where he will demonstrate his virtuosity. He struts to the spot where the music will begin.

Sitting in a photographic blind that looks like a cross between a backpacker's dome tent and an igloo, I know the bird is coming when I hear the crunching of claws and toes on dry leaves. He is a male ruffed grouse. Hidden by flimsy cloth and only a few inches away, I do my best to breathe softly and remain still. At first I see nothing. Then in a blur of gray, black, and brown, the grouse leaps onto the prostrate trunk of a dead fir.

The grouse comes to a halt on the broadest part of the bole, a slightly flattened place that offers him the right acoustics. He looks to the left, then to the right, then to the left again. On top of his head, a crest rises, adding a touch of the warrior to his otherwise civilized, tweed-and-necktie image. The bird droops his wings, and his throat opens and pulsates.

If there's a hen grouse watching, she must be impressed. Yet the best is yet to come.

The tail twitches up and down, spreading into a fan nearly as impressive as that of a turkey. I sense the grouse's agitation. He fairly twitches with anticipation for the performance that is about to begin, and no doubt in his grouse-like way he entertains hopes for an appreciative audience. Feet paw the log.

Suddenly it's happening. The grouse is facing me. Up go his wings, like the arms of an orchestra conductor about to commence a symphony. Then they sweep downward, chopping the air as if in a karate move. *Boom*! Once, then twice, the wings of the grouse thump the air smartly.

That's just the prelude. Now the wings pick up speed, chopping several times in swift but deliberate succession. *Boom-boom-boom-boom*. Quickly now, the bird segues to the breakneck speed of the symphony's third movement. The booming becomes a drum roll.

And then, as abruptly as the piece began, it's over. The musician bows, droops his wings, pants, and spreads his tail to its utmost. I want to clap but don't dare.

For several minutes, the grouse scans the forest ahead of him, his crest erect, an array of tiny white spots showing like sequins on his cheeks. I can guess what he's looking for: a hen, or hens. The bird isn't just making music. He's attempting to make time with every female grouse in the neighborhood.

Now he's at it again. Up go the wings, then down, first in slow measured beats, then accelerating to a speed where all I can see is a plump torso capped by a tiny head, bordered on each side by a blur the color of milked coffee.

It's one thing to watch such a performance on television, with your backside planted on a padded chair. It's quite another to sit deep in the woods in a blind, your feet in mud, mosquitoes drilling your flesh, your back and neck aching from too little movement in the cool and damp, your eyes glued not to a flickering image on a cathode ray tube but on a genuine, flesh-and-blood fellow traveler on our blue-and-green planet.

Boom-boom-boom goes the grouse. I feel its echo in my heart.

It's an afternoon in summer in the Adirondacks, and I'm listening. From all directions come sounds that tug my interest one way, then another.

There are birds—a song sparrow striking up the opening bars of a symphony Beethoven might wish he had written, a chestnut sided warbler that makes urgent, piping claims to love and territory, a robin that giggles, crows cawing, a red-eyed vireo asking half-hearted questions and then answering them before a rival male can intervene.

Tung! *Tung*! From a pond comes the blunt commentary of green frogs. In the background, I hear a drone of human conversation, the origin uncertain and the words too faint to make out.

The frog voices bring back the summer days of my childhood, before I knew the names of things. Bird sounds were just "chirping" then. Frogs were targets to be captured with hand or hook. We used to catch them for pets, press them into hard labor as fishing bait, or, if feeling particularly unforgiving, chop off their legs and persuade our elders to fry them in cooking oil.

Am I more sensitive today? Yes and no. Certainly, I'm more soft-hearted. The thought of hacking legs off an innocent frog revolts me.

Yet I am less sensitive, too. Often I know more but feel less. I can name every local species of frog by its love song, yet the days, the thrilling days, when I could spend hour after hour thinking only of frogs are behind me. My thinking ranges more widely than it used to, but I doubt that it plumbs more deeply. Some of the old intensity has been sacrificed to breadth.

Over the course of my life, my respect for other lives has risen and fallen, flowed and ebbed, swung left then veered right. As a tiny child, I was loath to kill anything, even a fly. Then I learned a hunter's pleasures and took up the fly swatter, becoming a serial killer of housefly and deer fly.

Today, halfway to ninety but with no assurance of getting there, I feel a sympathy for flies. A mosquito or blackfly that lands on my skin still feels the sting of my hand, but any insect not actively involved in assaulting me gets relocated rather than flattened. I think I know the reason. The older we grow the more sharply the brevity and preciousness of life are etched on our sensibilities. A fly's brief life can no longer be shortened lightly.

Do you pay attention to moths? They gather around our porch light at night, and I marvel at their variety. Each is so soft and delicate that handling them is nearly impossible without inflicting injury. As much as possible, we leave the light off. That way the moths can go about their proper business, rather than batter themselves against windowpanes or find their way into the house.

Of all the moths we've seen lately, the handsomest is the virgin tiger moth. It commands the attention with forewings boldly marked in black and white and hind wings, often concealed, colored flame orange dotted with charcoal.

Getting interested in moths this summer marks something of a return for me to innocence. As a little boy, I marveled at these winged marvels of the night. Then, like most people, I learned to ignore them, except for the occasional giant silk moth fluttering by on bat-sized wings. Now I *ooh* and *ahh* anew. Moths enchant me.

Interesting, isn't it? As children we strive so hard to be adults. Then, as adults, we go to sometimes embarrassing extremes to regain the excitement and wonder that came to us naturally as kids.

* * *

If you've ever paddled a canoe you've seen them: long, sinuous, attenuated green plants leading a dream-like existence, swaying with the current in flumes of cool water. What are they, exactly? That's what I want to know.

Last year and this, I've been wading into the water among them, running my fingers through their soft strands and probing for clues. I've learned that some of the plants branch and some don't, that all tend to be flaccid, yielding to the push of water rather than opposing it, and that despite a superficial commonality of appearance, each species has unique features.

They are strange, these retrograde water spirits. Millions of years ago, their ancestors liberated themselves from imprisonment in water and moved onto land, yet more recent evolution sent them backward. They retain the modern, terrestrial traits of flowering and seed-making while re-adapting to life in liquid. Compared to the stiffly erect plants most of us know, aquatic plants are laid-back. Rather than stand, they sprawl. They are never rigid. A typical aquatic plant goes and grows with the flow.

The first water plant I studied in the river that flows past our house appeared in patches averaging in area about the size of a sheet of plywood. The stuff was dark, and it branched. The leaves looked like bristles, but rather than being stiff, they were soft and supple. Among the stems, I found flowers that trailed to the surface on long thread-like filaments.

Knowing I'd have to scrutinize the plant closely to identify it, I uprooted a small sample and carried it home in a bucket. There, poring over several books, I was able to give the thing a name. It was common elodea, *Elodea canadensis*, a native aquatic plant often sold for rooting in fish tanks.

I spied my next conquest while wading through a bed of elodea. This plant grew beside the elodea but looked strikingly different. It had long, rubbery stems with heart-shaped leaves whose veins ran parallel to each other. The leaf-bases embraced the stems. A perusal of botanical manuals led me into the thicket known as *Potamogeton*—a genus of pondweeds notorious even among experts for their obscure diagnostic features and inconstant habits of growth.

Identifying a *Potamogeton* can challenge even an expert, and an expert I am not. I pulled the specimen out of the bucket again and again, scrutinizing it each time with a magnifying glass, then comparing what I was seeing to what the books told me I was supposed to see. Eventually I reached a conclusion. I had my hands on *Potamogeton richardsonii*, sometimes called clasping-stem pondweed or bassweed. Later, a botanist friend showed the plant to a colleague conversant with pondweeds, and my identification was affirmed.

Now I'm moving on to a new challenge. In the river grows a third water plant, just as conspicuous as elodea and clasping-stem pondweed and perhaps the most handsome of them all. Its leaves are several feet long and less than an inch wide. They look like ribbons of the most cheerful Granny Smith apple green. The ribbons move constantly, dancing to the rhythm of the current.

I'm waiting for a warm, sunny day. When one arrives, I'll slip into shorts, slip out of shoes, and wade into the river in search of a specimen. I've scanned the books and decided that the plant is almost certainly wild-celery, *Vallisneria americana*. Wild-celery has a peculiar method of pollination, one that makes sense only in water. Male flowers break off and drift upward. If all goes well, they bump into female flowers, which open for business on the water's surface.

When male meets female, pollen sticks to stigmas, and a new generation of wild-celery is born. Theirs is not a bad life. Beginning as seeds, they drift downstream, take root in some pleasant shallow spot, and spend the rest of their days lolling in the sunshine, cooled and caressed in a perpetually rolling whirlpool.

Amidst the mist of a rainy Adirondack summer, even the most sanguine among us complains about the weather. Rain on Monday gives way to clouds and showers on Tuesday, which in turn degenerate into gullywashers on Wednesday, drizzle all day Thursday, thundershowers on Friday, and occasional showers all through the weekend. Enough is enough! Still, the sky dribbles down in pieces.

Trying to cheer myself this morning, I ponder the fact that relentless rain of the sort we're having gladdens the lives of some living things. I don a raincoat and step out for a walk. My mission is to see who and what revels in the deluge.

Everywhere I turn, mosses look ebullient. Pincushion moss, which blanches in dry weather, covers broad swaths of the forest floor in cheery patches of lime. I've never seen the plant so radiant. Hair-cap moss also looks chipper. It stands a little taller than the average moss on any day, but today it seems more upright than ever.

Of course, these mosses have good reason to be perky. Their sex lives, and indeed their lives in general, depend on water falling from above. They possess no roots to suck up water from the soil, and sperm produced by their male parts must have water to swim through in order to reach the female places where eggs are cradled. No doubt, this year's rainy July and August represent a wild, wonderful summer of love.

The ferns in the woods have a glow about them, too. Being more recently evolved and a bit more sophisticated than mosses, ferns have simple root systems, which give them a bit more independence. But still, fern love depends on rainfall, just like that of mosses and for the same reason. Maybe that's why every fern I gaze on today seems to be smiling.

Fungi also grow and reproduce best when it's wet. Among them, the soggy summer has produced a Renaissance. Spring and early fall generally summon swarms of mushrooms and their kin from the soil, and from rotting logs and other digestible places, with July and August marking a bit of a lull. Not so this year. I find fungi everywhere. There are white ones and orange ones, brown ones and a few *Amanita muscaria*, whose yellow caps bear loud white polka dots. I recognize several species and simply marvel at the rest. In every direction I turn, fungi bulge and encrust.

Wet weather is made for frogs but for some reason, even though I tramp through the haunts of American toads and wood frogs, I encounter none. But salamanders are another matter. The first log I peek under hides a resident red-backed salamander living in the moist, cozy shelter beneath it.

The red-back is an odd sort of amphibian. It defies the general amphibian pattern of laying eggs in a lake, river, pond, or puddle. Instead, it stays in the woods and passes from embryo to tadpole-like larva to miniature adult entirely inside its jelly-covered eggs. But the red-back still needs water. It flourishes only in damp soil. Without wet skin, the little salamander (at full size, about the length of your pinkie finger) suffocates. It has no lungs. Instead, it absorbs oxygen that dissolves in its mouth lining and on its moist epidermis.

I slog home in better spirits, convinced that a wet summer is not entirely a bad thing. My change of heart is timely. Tomorrow, the forecast promises rain.

"Looks like a damn *Salix*," growls botanist Ed "Ketch" Ketchledge, seventy-six, bending over a low-growing woody plant on the summit of Whiteface Mountain. The living legend, retired from his long-time teaching position at the State University of New York's School of Environmental Science and Forestry, is showing my friend Wayne Gall and me some of the unique plants that live on mountaintops. By "*Salix*" he means "willow." By prefixing the genus name of willows with an expletive, Ketch is venting the exasperation even experts encounter when trying to tell one willow from the next.

At one point, I look up to see Ketchledge silhouetted against the overarching blue sky, all the world beneath him. He looks like an Adirondack version of Lawrence of Arabia, wild, defiant, blazing with the life energy that merely smolders in the rest of us. Dressed entirely in green, Ketch could be the Green Man, the "Father Nature" of pre-Christian Europe.

Ed Ketchledge has been studying alpine vegetation on eastern mountain summits since the late 1940s. Among Adirondack residents and visitors interested in nature, he's a legend. I first heard of him in the early 1980s, and I'd been wanting to meet him ever since.

The damn *Salix* turns out to be the species known as *uva-ursi*, which translates directly into the common name, bearberry willow. It hugs the ground, as different from a tall, riverside willow tree as a mouse is from an oversized rodent like the beaver. The leaves are waxy and small, adaptations that help bearberry willow endure in a windy, rocky environment where rain comes often but moisture is difficult to retain.

"Over here," calls Ketchledge. This time he's found a rare cousin of dandelions and asters called Boott's rattlesnake-root, or *Prenanthes bootii*. The plant takes its name from John Wright Boott, a pioneer in the study of alpine plants who roamed the White Mountains of New Hampshire during the nineteenth century.

The rattlesnake-root isn't much to look at—drab, dusty, its leaves arrowhead-shaped and flowers gone to seed. The people milling around the summit today (and every day the Whiteface Mountain road is open) probably have no idea they're trampling it and other rare plants. As Ketchledge explains, that's a serious problem.

He shows us signs that have been installed to alert visitors to the presence of the rare plants and points out spots where he and helpers rebuilt eroded areas with rocks and grass. Without meaning to do harm, people step on the plants, Ketchledge tells us, destroying not only the vegetation, but also the precious soil in which they grow.

Unlike many scientists, Ketchledge goes out of his way to educate the public. For decades, he has led walks introducing participants to the beauty of alpine plants. In every outing, he talks about conservation. Hikers can help protect alpine plants, he says, by keeping their feet on bare rock when they visit summits, avoiding patches of mountain soil which are easily eroded, and above all by stepping around the plants.

"Here's *Euphrasia*, or eye-bright," says Ketch. We tower over a delicate wisp of a plant, little more than an inch high, with tiny purple flowers. Although the eye-bright isn't as rare as some of the other plants we find, the old man of the mountain clearly relishes seeing it in bloom.

Between spurts of walking, Ketch catches his breath. "I took a bullet through a lung during the War," he said, referring to a close call in the mountains of Italy during World War II. "Now I have emphysema." He tells us he feels lucky to be alive.

Wayne and I feel lucky, too. We've joined the circle of people who cannot imagine the Adirondacks without this lover and defender of humble plants. There's gotta be a "Ketch."

Walking a trail at the Wawbeek Resort this morning, a breeze off Upper Saranac Lake tickling the back of my neck, I become aware of a subtle but persistent and repetitive sound: a sound of leaves, of leaves rustling, rustling all around me. I look up. In every tree, leaves tremble.

I find myself thinking about—well, truth be told, I find myself thinking about nothing. As the logical functions of my brain switch off, I enter an acute sensory state. Thoughts drain away, leaving only perceptions.

Of those perceptions, the soft stirring of maple, beech, and birch leaves and the quiet, persistent shivering of hemlock boughs make the deepest impressions. Wind stirs them, and they vibrate, and the vibrations send coded messages through the air, and my ears receive the code, and they translate it into their own code, and the code races along neural pathways to my brain, and my brain takes the code and deciphers it, and finding the message of sufficient interest, interrupts the babble of information flooding in from nerve endings in my eyes, nose, ears, tongue, and fingertips. "Er, pardon me," says a group of cells in my ears, "but if we may cut in, the leaves of the trees are rustling, and you may want to pay attention."

I listen. The listening pulls the plug on other brain functions, my thinking mind goes dark (in a pleasing sort of way), and a sense of calm comes over me from head to toe. Of course, if hurricane winds were screaming through the woods, I'd experience a different effect.

What's the big deal? I admit that nature affords more dramatic sounds than the quiet murmurings of leaves fluttering in a summer breeze. I am certainly not the first to notice them. But it occurs to me, after my analytical mind switches back on, that absolutely everything in nature is significant in one way or another if only we take note.

What is going on up in the treetops? Leaves are yielding to the breeze's push rather than opposing it. That's why the messages I receive are ones of peace rather than conflict.

The leaves of maples, birches, and beeches all consist of wide blades borne on thin, flexible stalks called petioles. Even hemlocks present their tiny needles to the world on stems rather than attach them directly (as balsam firs do) to the twig. Maples, birches, beeches, and hemlocks are not closely related to each other. Yet here they are, all exhibiting the same adaptation to life in a windy wood.

Surely, there's an important advantage in it, this linking of soft leaf to hard twig via supple petiole. But what can it be?

There are several possible answers. Petioles allow leaves to flutter more than they would without them. The yielding to the wind which fluttering represents may help leaves hang on rather than break off. In matters of leaf attachment, rigidity is probably not a virtue.

There's also the matter of gas exchange. Leaves pull carbon dioxide out of the air while breathing out oxygen. A fluttering leaf is probably better able to accomplish these tasks than a leaf that stands still.

Think, too, of heat. Leaves exposed to bright sunlight might well broil on a summer day like this one. Fluttering undoubtedly helps leaves keep cool, both by promoting evaporation and by encouraging direct heat transfer into each passing breeze.

I wonder, too, if the movement of leaves doesn't impart some small advantage in discouraging certain kinds of insects. Leaf-eating bugs must work harder hanging onto shaking leaves than holding onto ones that never move.

Yet none of this enters my mind, at least at first. For a few transcendental moments, the moving leaves and I drift together in a single stream of consciousness, and I savor the free and easy ride.

High, tinkling notes rain from the sky. Puzzled, I peer through the grid of limbs, twigs, and leaves overhead to see if I can spy the singer. All I glimpse through a blue window is a brown shape, plummeting earthward like an autumn leaf. The outburst grows louder as the shape grows nearer. It concludes with a snatch of *teacher-Teacher-TEACHER*!

The bird is an ovenbird, a wood-warbler named for its habit of roofing over its ground nest like a Dutch oven. Why does this particular ovenbird, generally a singer of the forest understory, forsake the relative safety of the trees, where its camouflage serves it well, to climb into the lethal realm of falcons, and there broadcast such a clamor?

In the animal world, risky behavior tends to be indulged in for good reason. Perhaps the ovenbird is showing off for rivals, or for a mate or prospective mate. Maybe competing male ovenbirds are only put in their places by an occasional hell-for-leather stunt flight. Then again, perhaps it's choosy female ovenbirds who demand it, ones who require of their mates death-defying professions of devotion. Perhaps it's both.

The ovenbird stages the play just once in my presence, then goes back to its usual practice of singing from low limbs ten or twenty feet above the ground. But I'm delighted to have witnessed something I've never seen before, even though I've spent dozens of hours watching ovenbirds. I like it when an old dog teaches me a new trick.

Nearly twenty years ago, I first witnessed a warbler's flight song. The daredevil then was not an ovenbird, but a close cousin of it called the worm-eating warbler. With the expert coaching of my friend, John Van Valkenburg, who possesses an almost clairvoyant ability to discover hidden birds' nests, I'd found a grass-lined cup full of baby worm-eating warblers and spent a week photographing it.

Days passed, and I thought I'd seen all that the birds could show me. They flitted through the forest, snatched up assorted bugs, spiders, and inchworms, and stuffed the tidbits down the throats of their nestlings. They carried away diaper-like fecal sacs, performed their own bodily functions, and took time out now and again to perform and appreciate metallic, insect-like trills by the male. Then, one placid evening, Father Warbler seemed to lose his mind.

He turned his back on home and family, and like a gray-haired banker or insurance agent discovering his inner teenager, flew up through the trees and into the sky beyond. There he commenced a performance much like the ovenbird's, falling to earth at its conclusion. He did the whole show two or three times, then, having gotten the whole thing out of his system, settled back into the sedately busy life of the working parent.

A hundred years ago, naturalists such as John Burroughs offered poetic explanations for these flights of fancy. More recently, Lang Elliott served up an entire chapter on aerial songs and published reactions to them in his extraordinary book *Music of the Birds: A Celebration of Bird Song*, published by Houghton Mifflin. Burroughs called such atypical singing by a warbler an "air song" or "song of ecstasy." He believed that a surfeit of joy inspired it.

Who can say Burroughs is wrong? These days I witness a parallel in the behavior of our two-year-old son. Ned gets so happy sometimes when we take him outdoors that he runs forward, away from his parents, exultant, head and shoulders thrown back, singing and gurgling in pure joyous effusion. Witnessing this human flight song, like catching an ovenbird or worm-eating warbler in the act, is a rare treat—whatever it means.

The first morning I hear it, the sound penetrates the outer reaches of my consciousness. *Glug-glug-glug…glug-glug-glug.* Half awake, half listening to the morning chatter of birds trickling into the screened porch where I sleep, I catch the notes, full and round.

I hear them yet I don't hear them. Half of me remains asleep, and when I eventually lurch to my feet, the peculiar sounds are forgotten.

The second morning, the voice comes again. Exactly as it did the day before, the source speaks from afar, from across the lawn, from the far side of the road, from an obscure point deep in a thicket. *Glug-glug-glug…glug-glug-glug.*

This time, the sounds penetrate a middle layer of my consciousness, and I think to myself, in the way that one grapples awkwardly with things when half alert and half sleeping, that this is a new sound, a sound I haven't heard in a long, long time, and I should leap out of bed and play close attention to it. But I do not leap out of bed. I don't even open my eyes. I listen, absorb the notes without thinking, and drift back into general anesthetic slumber.

The third morning, long before the alarm clock blares, it comes again. *Glug-glug-glug…glug-glug-glug.* This time the mind reacts. I wake with a start, haul myself upright, and listen closely.

Glug-glug-glug…glug-glug-glug. The song, surely, comes from a bird. But what bird? The summer grows old, and the days of new birds arriving seem past us. Who, I wonder, among the usual suspects is speaking?

I scan the gray coils of memory and reach a conclusion. Despite the lateness of the season, the singer is, in fact, a new bird, a late-arriving wanderer. But which wanderer? I wipe the sleep from my eyes and ponder.

Glug-glug-glug…glug-glug-glug. The bird keeps calling. I'm lucky on that score. This is no hit-and-run sort of visitor. It stays in one place and sings over and over and over until the repetition grows maddening.

Suddenly the answer I've been seeking bobs up out of a dark mental pool. Of course! Three mornings in a row, I've been awakened by a black-billed cuckoo, a bird I haven't seen or heard in a dozen years.

That's how it goes with our northeastern cuckoos, the black-billed and the yellow-billed. You go years without hearing one, and suddenly, they spew out their guttural, gulping songs and won't let you sleep. In the Adirondacks, black-billed cuckoos are more often heard than yellow-billed cuckoos. Black-bills tend to cough out guttural notes on a steady pitch in clusters of three, four, and five. Yellow-bills, more common to the south, generally broadcast a long series of glottal sounds, slowing down dramatically toward the finish.

If I remember correctly, the last time I set eyes on a black-billed cuckoo was in the 1980s. A full-blown gypsy moth infestation was underway in the Hudson Valley, where I lived at the time. Cuckoos appeared in great number to raise young and feast on the caterpillars.

Most birds eat few if any hairy caterpillars because the "hairs" are actually spines laced with chemical irritants. But the cuckoo has a way of circumventing the problem. It gorges on the caterpillars, insensitive to their nettlesome secretions, and when the spines accumulate in the stomach in great number, the cuckoo coughs up a disposable stomach lining. Out go the prickers, and in goes another juicy meal of caterpillars.

This year in our part of the Adirondacks, I've noticed more than the usual abundance of eastern tent caterpillars and forest tent caterpillars. I suspect the black-billed cuckoo that's been singing to us mornings has noticed the abundance, too. Now the bird has decided to see if it can capitalize on the discovery. It's singing for a mate. No doubt a hearty meal of moth larvae stirs a cuckoo's libido.

If the bird wakes me tomorrow morning, I'll pull on a pair of shoes and see if I can find it. The black-billed cuckoo is an elegant bird, sleek of torso and long of tail, with red ringing its eyes. The red gives the bird a bloodshot and dissipated look, as if it has squandered its good looks and talents on too much romance and too little sleep. All the same, I'll be glad to catch a glimpse.

There's something unsettling about selling passion for a price. I live in the Adirondack Mountains, and there I ply what may very well be the oldest of local professions: leading paying customers into the woods. Before hordes of loggers came to these forested slopes there were guides, who with varying degrees of skill and aplomb took people out to hunt and fish and soak up the mountain air. Unlike the guides of old, I carry with me into the woods a college diploma, a pair of lightweight high-resolution roof-prism binoculars, and a guiding license issued by the New York State Department of Environmental Conservation. I know little about hunting and fishing. But I can spin a trailside yarn of flora, fauna, and history that blends old-fashioned woods experience with the gleanings of modern science.

The thing is, I feel queasy about charging substantial sums of money to show people my favorite birds, beavers, wildflowers, groves of old-growth trees, salamanders, and hidden corners of the Adirondacks' six million acres. In an ideal world, I'd do it for nothing. My qualms would evaporate like morning rain on a hot summer day. But I have promises to keep and children to feed. These all require income.

So off I go, into the woods, for a price. On the best days, and there are many of them, I feel like paying my clients for the day's outing, rather than the other way around. I find that people who like nature are people that I like. A few minutes after initial introductions, we're glorying together in the wonders of the North Woods and hobnobbing like old friends.

What do we talk about, deep among the spruce, pine, and balsam? Two weeks ago, I guided a couple from North Carolina who showed a keen interest in everything, but most of all wanted to know about Adirondack wildflowers. So flowers we sought. Over the course of three hours we found enough to keep us interested: orchids such as rose pogonia, calopogon, and white-fringed; the weird parasol-like blooms of pitcher plants; and pretty but ordinary things such as white wood asters and dew-drop.

The husband and wife had traveled widely in New Zealand, as have I. So we talked during the in-between times of tree-ferns and kiwis, of the reptile called the tuatara, and of the taste of good New Zealand mutton. I had a grand time. My companions, I think, passed the day pleasantly, too.

On another walk, that ever-fascinating subject, sex, engaged the interest of the group, so we spent a good deal of time discussing the reproductive habits of mosses and ferns and the trees that towered over them. All seemed amazed by the fact that plants produce sperm and eggs much like animals do, and that plants nurture fertilized eggs inside maternal tissues in what might be termed a botanical pregnancy. The lack of a microscope prevented us from actually seeing these things, but no one minded. It was a gorgeous day to be out walking, cool and sunny, and we were able to examine some of the flowers, cones, and pregnant ovaries that get the job done.

All in all, I relish the work. I meet the nicest, most thoughtful of people, and by leading them into the labyrinthine woods and providing a mix of science, entertainment, companionship, and direction, I earn my daily bread. Still, there are moments when I feel uneasy. After all, I sell my passion for the pleasure of others, and I'd really prefer to do it for free.

As I lie awake, kept conscious past midnight by the whining of a ravenous Adirondack mosquito, I ask myself, "What good are these flaming vampires that invade our house, patrol our bedroom, and torture us at all hours?"

An answer comes swiftly. Mosquitoes are no good at all. The world would be better off without them.

Despite the prospect of blood loss, sleep finds me. In the morning, I awake with a healthier attitude. Of course, mosquitoes are good for something, I say. But what?

I make an earnest effort to think of the insect's positive points. After a couple of hours, I concede that the effort has failed. So I unleash my mind and let it chase off in other directions.

Aha! A fresh question comes to mind. What good are people?

Well, you might say. People feel. People think. Our emotions and consciousness of the world elevate us above other living things or at least make us stand apart.

Humbug. Tell this to a woodchuck and see what kind of reaction you get.

People good, mosquito bad? It would make an interesting election. Put the issue to the greater community of life on earth and let it decide: which is the baddest, meanest, most loathesome creature in the world, the mosquito or the human being? The result, I fear, would not be in our favor.

That is not to say that we *Homo sapiens* should all be flattened with gigantic flyswatters, although there are species that might take this position if they had a mind to. Like you and I, mosquitoes have intrinsic value. It's just hard for us to fathom what that value is.

Are you on the South Beach diet? The Atkins? The mosquito is your friend. It offers a sort of matching grant program in which you give away flesh and blood in order to help female mosquitoes grow their eggs.

Here are the details. Mosquitoes invade the house. By day you chase them, and by night you toss and turn in bed, writhing to the whine of their beating wings. Result? You burn body fat.

The mosquitoes also spirit away blood. It isn't much, but hey, when trying to lose weight, every drop helps.

Sure, mosquitoes may infect you with West Nile virus or equine encephalitis, but there's no gain without risk. Those of us who live in the Adirondacks can at least take heart that the odds are in our favor. As an outdoorsman who refuses to anoint himself with DEET, I've suffered thousands of mosquito bites and—knock on pine—not yet contracted anything awful.

Mosquitoes help deter developers from building in wetlands and overnight guests from staying too long in our bug-haunted house. They prevent me from spending entire weekends working on home-improvement projects and drive off people canoeing the Saranac River who decide that our lawn is a nice place to picnic.

These things recommend mosquitoes to us, although they really need no defense. Mosquitoes live for their own sakes, and so of course do we.

God has been accused of having an "inordinate fondness" for beetles. Perhaps there's truth to it. According to Richard White's *Beetles: A Field Guide to the Beetles of North America*, of the million or so species of animals recognized by science, approximately 300,000 are beetles. Estimates of the total number of living beetle species on Earth go as high as ten million.

I admit I've been guilty of avoiding beetles. I either look the other way when I see one or pronounce every insect with a forward pair of wings modified into protective covers for the rear pair "a beetle of some kind" and leave it at that. This is a shameful way for a naturalist to behave.

But nature, it seems, has other plans for me. Today it delivers onto the doorstep of our house in the Adirondacks a live beetle, so big and provocative that I cannot resist bringing it indoors for a look.

From the outer reaches of the creature's elaborate mouthparts to the culmination of its handsomely rounded abdomen, it measures about an inch and an eighth. It has tiny club-like antennae and is utterly bereft of color, or to put it another way, it's as black as bat wings. Grooves in the beetle's wing covers, or elytra, give it the same slick, leathery, finely wrinkled look that characterizes bats at rest and traditionalist riders of Harley Davidson motorcycles. When I look closely, I catch a flash of blue, a prismatic hint of iridescence.

What sort of beetle is it? As one of my Australian friends might say in familiar company, buggered if I know. Alone at the examining table in my office and lab, I find the courage to confront my ignorance. If, after a struggle to identify it, the beast remains simply "a beetle of some kind," the insect (if not my naturalist friends) can be counted on not to laugh.

Off the shelf come three books offering hope of illumination. One is White's *Field Guide*. The second is Lorus and Margery Milne's *Audubon Society Field Guide to North American Insects and Spiders*. The third is an out-of-print classic, my favorite insect book, Lester Swan's and Charles Papp's *Common Insects of North America*. With a bit of work and luck, perhaps I'll be able to at least name the family of beetles to which this gentleman or lady belongs.

Starting with Swann and Papp, I pick through page after page of beetle illustrations and descriptive text. The search begins on page 330 and might stretch all the way to page 507 and back again, but I gasp in delight after 109 pages. There on page 439 appears, or seems to appear, the very beetle that keeps tumbling over on its back inside the plastic magnifying box in which I've detained it for questioning.

Can it really be so easy? I scan hundreds of illustrations and reams of text. To my astonishment, it seemed that for once in my life I've identified a beetle, and not just to family. The black passalus, bess beetle, horned passalus, or patent-leather beetle (it has many names) has no close look-alikes in eastern North America.

Now that I know the beetle's name (scientists call it *Odontotaenius disjunctus*) I learn what it does when not plodding across doorsteps. The bess beetle inhabits rotting logs. There it wolfs down decaying wood, presumably to be digested by helpful bacteria in its gut. Apparently, bess beetles are good parents. They chew wood to soften it, then feed the stuff to their grubs.

Feeling pleased with myself and pleased with the beetle, too, I set it free.

Next time I go to the woods, I'll watch and listen. Listen, because Swan and Papp report that the bess beetle is "said to communicate by stridulating."

What insects say by rubbing body parts against each other no one really knows. In the case of the bess beetle, it's probably along the lines of "Hey Honey, why don't you come up to my decaying stump and see me sometime." The propositions must be warmly received. As I said at the outset, there are an awful lot of beetles.

This Adirondack summer morning begins with the faint siren-like whine of mosquito, homing in on carbon dioxide spilling from my nostrils and oozing from my pores. I lie asleep one moment, angrily awake the next. The little vampire floats into view with landing gear dangling. With a satisfying clap of the hands, I send it back to the collective unconscious.

A few minutes later, I step out the kitchen door. My mission is to extricate the bird feeder from a metal garbage can in the shed and hang it where chickadees, purple finches, and nuthatches will find it. The feeder spends each night in the shed as a precaution against visiting black bears.

I am a few strides from the house when I feel the first insect mouthpart rasp into my flesh. Almost instantly, the sensation multiplies. Someone watching me from a distance would see a man suddenly demented, slapping himself violently from head to ankle.

This second attack is mounted by blackflies. For six weeks, or thereabouts, they render one of the finest times of year at our Adirondack home a trial to be endured. After passing their larvalhoods in the cool oxygenated stream that pours across our property, they boil out of the water and rise into the air, the females thirsting for blood.

In me they find it aplenty. I count the ruby-red abrasions on my skin where blackflies have scraped and lapped—more than a dozen on my left arm, about the same on my right, six or eight on each temple, another dozen on my neck. Unseen on my nape, scalp, and the backs of my ears, the majority of wounds defy tallying.

At midday, I venture out for more than an hour. It's a brave and foolish act. Bugs are instantly upon me— mosquitoes drilling through my clothing, blackflies hacking at unprotected flesh, and a new marauder, the deerfly, circling around me in great loops until it tears a small hole in the back of my neck.

What to do? I might scream. I might sprint for the river, submerge, and try breathing through a hollow reed. But there's work to be done. So I put on a long-sleeve turtleneck shirt, rub citronella on my hands, and pull a hat with insect netting down over my head.

Now the insects can only torment with their buzzing, or so I think. Somehow a blackfly slips under the veil to bite me on the right cheek, and before I can turn the other cheek, a plump deerfly joins it. With relish, I crush the deerfly between a thumb and my jawbone. Meanwhile mosquitoes demonstrate the ease with which they can stab through fabric.

At last it's bedtime. After a day in our mountain paradise, I crawl into bed. We sleep on a porch, and for as long as three seconds it's a joy to hear night sounds and feel the cool of the evening drifting through the window screens.

Unfortunately, the breeze also brings no-see-ums, tiny monsters that inflict the most painful bites of all. No-see-ums are named for an obvious reason. They're a kind of fly, or Dipteran, placed by scientists in the family *Ceratopogonidae*.

I'm not sure what "*Ceratopogonidae*" means in English, but for me, at the end of a long day spent nourishing insects, it translates as hell on two wings.

Sometime in August, I always notice. Insects buzz, cars roar, and airplanes drone. But songbirds are silent, and the soundscape seems empty without them.

Through April, May, June, and July, every Adirondack woodland and field serves as an amphitheater in which birds of camouflage and color carol their desires for love and territory. Most of the singers are males, although female cardinals, orioles, purple finches, and a few others announce the wants of the feminine. Then it happens. Almost as if someone has switched off a stereo, the music dies with hardly a whimper.

If I listen closely, of course, I can still find the odd bird singing here and there, and a few late-breeding species such as the American goldfinch whistle and warble as exuberantly as ever. But by and large, quietude prevails. Birds either don't sing, or they sing less, or they melodize in whispers.

Why the change? Songbirds open their mouths and crow for a variety of reasons, chief among them the declaration and defense of breeding territories and the advertisement for mates. With the end of the nesting season, these needs fade away. No longer are territories as vital as they used to be. The lonely hearts club band loses its reason to play.

The sudden silence always seems dramatic. Without bird song electrifying the air wherever I turn, woods and meadows that felt cheery and welcoming turn somber and cold. Even those of us who can't tell a song sparrow's aria from a blue jay's cry probably still sense a void.

As August progresses, insects make up for some of the loss. Field crickets chirp, cicadas buzz, and snowy tree crickets trill at night by the hundreds of thousands. Over much of the country, katydids of various species commence an annual rhythmic chatter. Yet bug noise lacks the soulfulness of bird song, and I always lament what's missing.

In spring and early summer, my mind swirls with thoughts of beginnings, of new life and expanding possibilities. Bird songs play in the background like a brass band, their anthems jaunty and bold. Then at midsummer, the music fades and the tenor of my thinking changes. I begin thinking of endings: of seasons come and gone, of people and places nearly forgotten, of leaves and flowers that wither.

How many more years will I hear the hermit thrush sing moonlight sonatas in Adirondack hemlock groves, or cheer as the rose-breasted grosbeak whistles in the dawn? I have no idea. But I do know this. With the birds' summer concert series over, I feel grateful to have been around to catch the show, and I take my place in line for another year.

Floating in a kayak down a murky, leech-infested stream on a muggy afternoon, I am dazzled by color and form.

First there are damselflies, hovering and darting over the water, perching on alders and grasses that grow along the banks. Occasionally one alights on my yellow synthetic bow.

Thanks to Ed Lam's excellent field guide, *Damselflies of the Northeast*, I am able to give names to two of the damselflies. One is relatively substantial, the other wraithlike and barely large enough to see.

The big damselfly, which alights with wings folded over its back (a damselfly trademark), has broad black wings. Its body parts are colored such a luminous and metallic green that they glow like neon. These are ebony jewelwings. Even the kids paddling with me, more interested in looking for moose and bears along the banks than in savoring little treasures, gasp in admiration when I point to one.

Less eye-catching, but no less pretty, is the eastern forktail damselfly, toothpick-thin, clear of wing, and so delicate that one might be tempted to deny its existence. Lime-green dots the face and stripes the thorax, and the long dark abdomen culminates in a cheery dab of summer-sky-blue.

Bright as the damselflies may be, an even showier color catches our eyes along the banks. It's the flaming crimson of the cardinal-flower, a plant named for the Catholic prelates whose robes are similarly pigmented. Cardinal-flower is a native member of the group of plants known as *lobelias*.

There's something strange about cardinal-flower. Its color is so vibrant that when you look at it, your eyes go fuzzy. The plant seems to broadcast color, not just possess it. "It is not so much something colored," wrote the naturalist John Burroughs of cardinal-flower more than a century ago, "but color itself."

Cardinal-flower tends to grow spottily, even in good, muddy streamside habitat. Yet here it pokes up every dozen feet or so, one after another after another. We see fifty or more. Hummingbirds, fanatical about the color red, are this lobelia's best-known pollinators. We watched for hummers but none ever appears.

This is a short voyage. We drift in our little flotilla of three kayaks about a quarter mile downstream, then swing into the current and paddle back toward our starting point.

While the others flex their muscles and shoot ahead, I paddle half-heartedly, scanning the banks for further discoveries. Soon I find a pleasing sight: a tight group of turtleheads.

These are not the sort of turtleheads that give purpose to the necks of turtles. They're wildflowers. Turtleheads look nothing like cardinal-flowers. They grow in the same places and stand about the same height (two feet or thereabouts), but when evolution handed out color, cardinal-flower got more than its share and turtleheads all but nothing. If a turtlehead possesses any color at all, it's merely a hint of pink. Typically, the blossoms are white.

Turtlehead (like cardinal-flower) produces blooms that start off in male form, dispensing pollen, and then ripen into pollen-catching, seed-producing females. It's a practical arrangement for promoting cross-pollination and discouraging botanical incest. There's nothing pretty about turtlehead flowers. Crowded atop a leafy stem, they're fleshy and grotesque. Still, the sight of them is to be savored. When turtleheads leave us, so does summer.

There's a silvery quality to the moon-glow this August night. It covers every object in the landscape with a cool icy light. The trees and grass appear frosted, yet the atmosphere feels like the inside of an oven. It's too hot to sleep, too hot to think.

So I head down to the Saranac and drift. Lying back on soft water, I let the flow carry me along. I'm a canoe: head the bow, toes the stern, together sliding downstream.

Nearby, I hear something stir. Ripples make waves in air and water. It's a muskrat, perhaps, or a beaver.

I feel a stab of fear. Then it passes as automatically as it came. Sharks are one thing, rodents another. Nothing to be afraid of here as long as I remember how to swim.

As I float along, I think of the fish swimming beneath me. Bullheads are down there, feeling their way along the mucky bottom with sensitive whisker-like organs called barbels. The barbels look like mere adornments but to the fish they're much more important. With them, a bullhead finds its sustenance: worms, insects, crayfish, leeches, whatever piques its interest.

There are probably pike, too, the largest of them perhaps half as long as I am, sunfish, suckers, chunky bass, all going about the business of being fish. It must be wonderful to be always cool, forever wet. Yet I pity my piscine companions their inability to enjoy terra firma.

Do the fish gaze up at the banks, longing for what they cannot have? I doubt it. Through a lens of shifting, clouded water, they gain an uncertain view of cardinal-flower, pickerelweed, and bulrush. To them the world beyond the river must seem like a dream, partly real, partly imagined.

In the distance I hear barking. It could be a dog; that's the likely explanation. Yet at long distance, barred owls sound like German shepherds. I choose to think I'm hearing owls.

I drift under a bridge. Suddenly the handful of stars that lay scattered across the humid, moonlit sky yield to straight lines and blackness. Barn swallow nests lie empty now. Above me all is silence.

Now I metamorphose from canoe to buoy. I'm bobbing in the current, blinking water from my eyes. To my right I spy boulders, amorphous black shapes trimmed along the edges with quicksilver.

As I reach out for rock, my fingertips touch warmth and solidity and my feet probe deep into muck. Somewhere nearby, a snapping turtle undoubtedly lurks. I picture it, motionless and stoic. The turtle accepts my presence without protest. It could bite me but never does.

I crawl out, like some primordial beast rising from the ancestral ooze, dripping, wobbly on my feet, taking a few moments to adjust to the change of element. It was a good swim. And it's good to be on land.

Am I dreaming? Summer nights have a way of feeling like dreams, of stirring up so many emotions and associations that the mind goes cloudy, and you grow uncertain of your bearings. What's real and what's imagined blend. Past and present mix with the future. You live in the moment, in all moments, like a fish or a muskrat, eating, drinking, waking, sleeping, for however long it lasts.

Autumn

An autumn morning in the Adirondacks sometimes makes me think of another fall—the fall of ancient Rome.

They begin with promise. With nearly the speed of chariots, they burst upon the forest and turn it into something new. Exploding open here, unfurling there, they announced that spring has arrived and a new regime holds dominion over the landscape.

For a time, it seems like the empire will last forever. A magnificent system of aqueducts hauls up moisture from the depths of the earth and carries it high into the society's many branches. A cool shade spreads over the land, and riches are gathered and stored.

Then, perhaps inevitably, sloth and corruption creep in. Extraordinary growth turns to excessive decay as some citizens grow pale and flabby while others deck themselves in gaudy colors. There is not one deathblow but many. Like barbarian invaders of old, winds sweep in and sack the sorry vestiges of empire. The end comes not with a bang but with a flutter like the flapping of a million butterflies.

The story repeats itself in Adirondack forests every year. The players are the leaves of deciduous trees, whose empire of green rises swiftly in April and May but succumbs every autumn to shortening days and the steady onset of cold.

I spy the first fall color in late July. (The calendar's assertion that autumn begins on September 21 is absurd.) This is a time when red maple trees and shrubs called hobblebush foretell the future with touches of red that multiply with passing weeks. A few scarlet leaves here, a limb's worth of crimson there, these stoic fortunetellers hint at the debacle to come.

By late August, the bright greens of May are merely a memory. Leaves have lost their luster, chartreuse has matured to olive, and discolored spots and holes caused by pathogens, insects, and ozone pollution impart a look of fatigue and surrender.

Slowly at first, but with increasing speed, deciduous trees sever the ties to their leaves. Deprived of moisture and denied the raw materials from which green pigments are made, the leaves blanch. Underlying yellow pigments are revealed, and, depending on the species involved, new red and purple pigments form. As a result, the empire collapses in a reckless feast of color.

In the sensibly-named red maple, red pigment predominates. In its cousin the sugar maple, red and orange unite in a conflagration of orange. In the white ash, mauve and purple arise, although their reign is tragically brief.

Birches yellow, beeches mellow from gold to copper, and oaks either brown directly or present brief intermediary displays of yellow, pink, or red. The peak of autumn color in the Adirondacks is hotly debated, but most would agree it comes sometime in mercurial October.

By mid-November, the empire lies in ruins. The culture of leaves that flourished extravagantly in June and July lies moldering. All that remains is architecture—grand columns, sweeping arches, and the intricate pattern of twigs that will endure through the Dark Age to come.

October is my birth month. I was born one cool morning three days before Halloween and have had a warm spot in my heart for the month ever since.

Maybe it's the colorful leaves. September brings the deep ruby reds of red maples, but October is the month when those embers are fanned to flame as a wave of sugar-maple-orange blazes across the hillsides. Other fractions of the year please the eye, but none excites the retina quite like October.

Orange is the month's signature color, and it seems to drip off the trees and paint the skins of pumpkins. Venture into farm country among the Adirondack foothills, and you're likely to find heaps of ripe pumpkins for sale at every turn, most of them destined for afterlives as jack-o-lanterns.

The inside of a typical American pumpkin is as orange as the outside. One of my favorite things to do is cut a pumpkin into chunks, scoop out the seeds, bake the flesh until soft, and incorporate it into a pumpkin pie. Cookbooks usually recommend homogenizing the mush in a ricer or blender, but don't be foolish. Why turn your pumpkin into stuff exactly like the mush that comes from a can? A certain stringiness to pumpkin flesh gives a pie made from it a delightful texture. You'll swear every forkful includes bits of coconut.

October is a wonderful time to appreciate warm weather. Balmy days in summer are easily cursed or taken for granted, but by the time October rolls around in our neck of the woods, you realize warmth is a limited resource. There's no weather quite as satisfying as the warmth and sunshine of a mild day in autumn.

Regarding October's position in the calendar, isn't it strange that the tenth month has a name incorporating the Latin "octo," meaning "eight"? There's a rational explanation. October was the eighth month in the early Roman calendar. Still, the odd numerology of the name makes perfect sense, for October is a month rich in mystery and haunted by the peculiar. It culminates in that most macabre of holidays, Halloween.

Halloween has become a lighthearted celebration of death, at least death as represented by ghosts and goblins. In the Adirondacks, the natural world has its equivalent. October frosts massacre the insects that made a symphony of the woods and fields during August and September. Those of us who are paying attention mourn the loss, yet we welcome it, too. As crickets and katydids grow silent and the last of our migratory birds wing off for the tropics, the first winter tourists begin to arrive by plane, train, and automobile. The local economy could not survive without them.

This morning, I stand high on a ladder, nailing rafters to the ridge beam of an old-fashioned timber frame, when I hear a sound that I can't quite put my finger on. I listen some more. Of course! It's the distant *thump-thump-thumping* of a ruffed grouse. Why is the bird drumming on an October day, long after the grouse-breeding season has expired? I have no idea.

October is a month when I think often and deeply about the passage of time. Seasons are always coming and going, but in October, as frosts march in and demolish the world as we have recently known it, there are sober reminders everywhere that all lives end in death, and that every day and every month are unique and will never be repeated again. When my birthday rolls around at the end of the month, I blow out candles, put cake in my mouth, and find the taste sweet and sour. I'm glad for all the Octobers I've enjoyed. But how many more can I look forward to?

This afternoon I march into a thicket on our eighteen and a half Adirondack acres to cut the last of the winter's firewood. We heat our house with a woodstove, and its pantry, the woodshed, is nearly full with split hardwood. Still, two dead birches rising out of a thicket call to me. If I cut and split them soon, the wood will be dry enough to burn by March or April, when our supply may well run short.

Hardly have I plunged into the tangle, which consists mostly of choke-cherry, than a glimpse of something stops me in my tracks. It's fecal matter, lying in an ample heap. The stuff glistens with moisture. Tiny flies circle the pile, and dozens upon dozens of cherry pits bejewel it.

I don't feel fear exactly, but a cloud of concern darkens my outlook for a moment. A black bear has left its calling card very, very recently.

Fresh bear sign always gives me pause, and it should. Although black bears rarely trouble humans and are vegetarians for the most part, they're still carnivores larger and faster than I am. Whenever I find bear spoor close to home, I'm reminded of a set of tracks neighbors made a plaster cast of. They showed their handiwork to a bear biologist, whose eyes bulged. The bear that had made the tracks weighed, he estimated, about 600 pounds. That's an animal I wouldn't want to meet at close quarters.

I look, listen, and sniff the air. No sign of a bear. Still, to be sure, I sing a few bars of "Home on the Range."

Eager to cut wood, I step over the scat, find my way to the first skeletal birch, and fell it. The tree isn't big, its girth a smidgeon less than that of the average utility pole. In twenty minutes, I have the whole thing sliced to length, and I'm ready to move to the second tree.

This is when I run into a second pile of bear excrement. Like the first, it is wet and fly-haunted and undoubtedly parted company with its creator no more than a few hours ago. I scan the sea of leaves around me and listen for the snap of a twig. Logically, I know that the bear, if present when I arrived, fled when I fired up the chainsaw. But there's more to such a situation than logic.

I see bears rarely, but often I find the great carnivore's spoor. The smooth gray bark of beech trees preserve claw marks where impatient bears have mounted to the treetops to eat nuts before they fall. Black cherry trees look roughed up where climbing bears have pried off scales of bark. And yesterday, I saw a hemlock with big flakes of bark missing where a bear frightened by a passing hiker had likely shinnied up to avoid confrontation.

The bear that puts me most on edge is the one I expect to surprise near our compost heap. I work in an outbuilding, and often, late at night and half asleep, I trudge past the compost as I make my way back to the house. Lately, I've taken to carrying a flashlight, and to greeting the theoretical presence. A surprised bear can be a dangerous bear, so I always say hello.

Out of a corner of an eye I catch the shape: robust of breast, long of tail, oriented not horizontally like the average songbird but erect in the manner of a raptor. The apparition sits perfectly still. A hundred yards away, I first notice only the contrast between it and a bare tamarack limb with bright sky behind it.

I bustle back to the house for binoculars. Crisp optics confirm my guess. The bird has bold eyebrow stripes and a blue-gray back. High in the tamarack, watching over our lawn, sits a goshawk.

As Debbie takes her turn with the binoculars, I keep an eye on the bird. I see it well enough to note a slight shifting of its dagger-toed feet. The goshawk seems uneasy.

What is the bird thinking? I can no more know the goshawk's thoughts than it can fathom mine. But ignorance never stops any of us. Regarding the feelings of others, we're born to speculate.

Does the bird find us threatening? Is that why it makes ready to fly? Goshawks have plenty to fear from humans. We shoot them, in defiance of the law, and we fell the forests in which they nest. Our speeding cars strike them on roads, detaching retinas, breaking wings, scrambling brains.

Does the goshawk think of its next meal? Here there is good cause to wonder. Does a raptor live entirely in the moment, thinking only of the things that pass before its eyes, or does it plan, plot, and look forward?

Questions spawn other questions. Does the goshawk perching here dread the hard weeks of winter that lie ahead? Does it gaze forward with optimism to April, to days of warmth, sunshine, and romance? I feel certain it does neither of these things. Circumstantial evidence paints the bird as a Zen Master. It isn't moping.

The past? I feel certain the goshawk wastes no effort looking back, back to its last failure (in hunting, raptors of all kinds fail more often than they succeed), or back to the days, a century ago and more, when now-extinct passenger pigeons abounded, and living for a goshawk in pigeon time was easy. We cannot be certain, but it seems likely that goshawks raised in high-rise nests are spared the odious lot of young humans, who spend their childhoods hearing from elders of the halcyon days before they were born.

Ignorance is both a blessing and a curse. Regret probably never haunts a goshawk's days, yet neither can it take lessons from its past in the way you and I can. Admire the bird, but do not romanticize it.

After enduring a minute or two of our scrutiny, the bird drops from the branch. Beating the air with sturdy wings, it passes overhead and plunges into the forest. Compared to most other hawks, the goshawk has short wings and an exceptionally long tail. These features combine to make it a nimble flier and lethal predator in a world of limb, trunk, and bramble.

Where will the goshawk sleep? Debbie and I know darkness will find us inside the house, snug under a quilt and blankets. But what about the bird? I picture it tucked inside a spruce or balsam, eyes closed, plumage fluffed like a down pillow.

What does a goshawk dream? The question provokes further speculation on this wintry autumn day as we set off for home on skis.

This morning I walk out the door and step into air so malodorous one might think a herd of horses has just thundered by, voiding a sea of manure in the process. Egad! What causes the smell?

To a naturalist who follows his nose, the answer is obvious. The season is autumn. Leaves lie moldering on the ground. Until a few days ago, hundreds of leaves festooned the twigs of a shrub called northern wild-raisin. Wild-raisin is a kind of viburnum, and when viburnum leaves rot, they reek to high heaven. (Cut the wood, and it stinks, too.)

I know where wild-raisins grow thickly near the house. For a bit of perverse fun, I walk closer to them, just to see if the stink gets stronger. It does, outrageously.

Disinclined to linger, I march down the road. A thin rain drizzles from the sky, drenching everything, including the top of my head. Safely away from the viburnums, I inhale a nose full.

In flows a mélange of scents. I can't identify a single one, save to say they rise from the soaked earth and undoubtedly include the exhalations of pseudoscorpions, sow bugs, millipedes, fungi, and bacteria. They represent the smell of decay—not the sort of decay that leads to grief, but a decay offering cheerful assurance that the carbon cycle rolls merrily along, and decomposers are on the job, turning yesterday's life into nourishment for tomorrow's.

As a teenager, I learned the pleasures of venturing out on damp days. The air folds around you like wet canvas, smells are magnified, and if you challenge your olfactory lobe to do its best, wonders are revealed. The lesson was taught to me by a basset hound named Freckles.

On I ramble. I'm halted along one stretch of our dirt road by a strong, delicious scent of balsam. Balsam fir grows almost everywhere in our cold corner of the Adirondacks. Why does its fragrance pool intensely in one spot? I'm mystified.

Seven houses appear, one by one, then vanish in my wake. The road slices into forest. Through a veil of drizzle

I plow ahead, snuffling. Life feels grand. I'd wag my tail if I had one.

I walk about a hundred paces, until a new scent finds its way to my muzzle. This one is most interesting. I advance slowly, step-by-step, until I determine by overshooting and backtracking the place where the sensation peaks.

Eureka! A red fox has passed here. The smell is telltale. It's vaguely skunk-like, but less acrid.

To Freckles, scents such as this held enormous allure. He would bury his nose in the leaf litter, no doubt zeroing in on the exact spot the fox anointed. Sometimes it would take several minutes and much persuasion to get him moving again.

I envy dogs their superior sniffers, but I refuse to concede them all the fun. My nose can't rival a basset hound's. Yet on damp days, I always like to take it for a walk.

Outside our back door, looming nearly as high as the roof of our house, lies a funeral pyre of bodies—the trunks of trees, shorn of their limbs, roots hacked off, as pathetically recumbent as beached whales. We bought the wood from a logger. The trees had died before he cut them, and the wood in their boles, pocked with rot and woodpecker holes, possessed little value as timber.

So the stuff came to us: two truckloads in all, lifted off the back of a flatbed truck with a knuckle boom that operates like a gigantic human arm. Now it's time for work.

With a chainsaw, whose teeth show no respect for bark or growth rings, I slice my way through the pile. An hour here, an hour there, I cut. When I have all the trunks reduced to stove-length, the next Herculean labor will commence:

splitting. Eventually, Debbie and I will stack the pieces in the woodshed, and one armload at a time they'll warm our house all winter.

Immersed as I am in wood and sawdust and the chainsaw's mighty roar, I find myself marveling at the stuff I'm preparing to reduce to heat, smoke, and ash. It's wood, of course: black cherry, sugar maple, and American beech for the most part, with the occasional bit of yellow birch and red maple thrown into the mix. We buy only hardwood from deciduous trees because it burns cleaner and longer and yields more heat per volume than the softwood from evergreens and tamaracks.

What are these trunks we're burning? They're just big sticks of candy, really. Like candy, you couldn't live on wood even though it represents solar energy captured and stored via that miracle known as "photosynthesis." Cellulose and lignin, its main components, are complex carbohydrates, which is to say, lengthy chains of sugars.

Just as you gain energy by breaking down sugars in your food, the fire in our woodstove dismantles the carbohydrates trees store in their wood. Instead of powering muscles, the energy liberated by the fire flows to us as heat. The heat warms the stove's cast-iron, and the iron radiates the heat that warms the house. Some of the fire's warmth goes to heating new wood, keeping the combustion reaction going. Wood burns as a gas, not as a solid. We witness this through the glass front of our stove. Jets of blue and yellow flame shoot out of the wood as if the stuff was pumped full of propane.

Alone in the house at times, I enjoy a companionship with the woodstove of a sort that one never develops with an oil- or gas-burning furnace. A furnace is generally locked away, hidden like an embarrassment in a basement or utility room.

The woodstove, by contrast, sits on a masonry throne in a conspicuous place in our kitchen. We make no secret of our relationship. The stove and I breakfast together, reconvene a few hours later for a hearty lunch, meet for dinner, and spend the evening before bedtime quietly digesting what fills our insides. The sugars, carbohydrates, and fats I metabolize and the cellulose and lignin burned by the stove are essentially peas from the same pod.

The use of the sun's energy to bind carbon, hydrogen, and oxygen atoms together in sugars and their derivatives is a trick no animal or fungus has mastered. But plants can do it, at least most of them, and so can certain protoctists (the kingdom of life that includes seaweeds) and cyanobacteria, formerly known as blue-green algae. Without the good work of these fellow, not-so-humble organisms, there would be no life on the planet as we now know it.

As I butcher the tree carcasses into bite-sized chunks to feed the stove, I feel grateful. These gentle giants of the plant world spent decades laboring in the sun, gathering carbon dioxide from the atmosphere and water from the earth. Steadily and incrementally, they laid down the products of their alchemy, putting on growth ring after growth ring, one per year, thick ones in good times, thin ones in bad. Carbohydrates made them grow ever wider, ever taller.

Now I dismantle and burn them. Carbon dioxide liberated by combustion flies into the air. There it is taken in by living trees. Steam and ash arise from combustion, too. The steam rises to nourish clouds. I haul the ash outdoors a bucket at a time to fertilize the soil in our vegetable garden.

Onward goes the eternal cycle. Atoms converge and disperse, lives begin and end, things grow and decay, cold turns to heat and heat to cold. Everything is there in the woodpile: the vast universe in rustic microcosm.

Grasping the meaning of death isn't an easy thing. I remember struggling with it as a kid, straining to understand how someone or something can be alive and aware one moment and inanimate and oblivious the next. Watching beloved pets, friends, and family members die brings the concept home painfully. Even so, death defies my comprehension.

Autumn, our beautiful, lethal Adirondack autumn, delivers individual extinction by the truckload. Every year I witness it with a touch of sadness. To avoid a funk, I remind myself that death is necessary, that without it there would be no new leaves in spring, no end to the population explosions of insects, no food for animals, no room for seeds to sprout and babies to grow. In the long view, death is life's good and necessary shadow.

But that doesn't mean I like to watch. A gorgeous black-and-yellow argiope spider spun an elegant web this summer in one of the hydrangeas lining our driveway. Today, the spider looks awfully subdued. Cool gray days and nights just above freezing have robbed it of vitality. Tonight, a hard frost is predicted. The argiope, a marvel of evolution and only a few months old, is almost certain to die an icy death.

I know the spider must perish sooner or later, that the natural order calls for argiopes to live in summer and die in autumn. Yet I will mourn its passing. I'm not sure why. Perhaps we mourn the deaths of others partly as a way of mourning ourselves. When the frosts of fate write our own obituaries, we won't be on hand to cry.

Yesterday I hung storm windows. On the east side of the house, I came upon a piñata-like nest built by a hornet known as the aerial yellow jacket, *Dolichovespula arenaria*. Clearly, the insects had been hard at work all summer. Their masterwork was now larger than a football. Six or eight hornets lingered around the threshold. Although they twitched as I nosed close, an attack never came.

I felt sorry for the hornets. For months they labored, chewing up bits of wood and regurgitating the pulp as paper, building a chambered nursery layer by corrugated layer. Their queen filled the structure with eggs, and workers raised the larvae that hatched from them. The workers defended the larvae against predators and parasites, too, week after toilsome week, sustaining themselves on insects and spiders they chased, stung, and devoured.

Now the hornets must die. Tonight's frost will kill them. I look up through binoculars to see how they're spending their last hours. A few mope around the threshold of the nest, perhaps drinking in the world one last time.

What's the meaning of it all—all this living, all this dying? Theological explanations do nothing for me. The only thing I'm certain of is that while absolute significance is hard to establish in the universe, relative meaning shouts from the treetops. Life serves the living, and death serves us, too.

Just now, I step outside and discover a dead cherry tree I haven't spotted before, bereft of branches, standing an easy stone's toss from my office door. The sight gladdens me because we're short of firewood. I feel guilty cheering the tree's demise. Still, its woody skeleton, seasoned on the stump, will help to keep my family and me warm this winter.

Which proves, at least to me, that the tree did not live and die in vain.

Naturalists are strange creatures. I know because every morning, shortly after I stumble from bed, I find one in the mirror. Hair askew, eyes bleary, he's not a pretty sight.

Naturalists mail peculiar things to each other. I know because last week I climbed a stepladder, scraped an enormous aerial yellow jacket nest from an eave on the east side of our house, and mailed it to my entomologist friend Wayne Gall in Buffalo. Surely, he would appreciate the contents.

Wayne had no warning the parcel was coming. Nor did he know that I had plopped the hornet's nest into the box without first taking the precaution of sealing it inside a plastic bag. Truth is, no sooner had I taped the box closed than I realized the error of my ways. Still, too short on time to consider packaging the nest over again, I proceeded straight to the post office.

My reasoning was that after a dozen or more hard frosts, not a single yellow jacket survived inside the nest. At the time, the notion seemed flawless.

United States Postal Service Priority Mail brought the package to Wayne's office in two days. There, on a day that began routinely, my friend sliced through the packaging tape. He did not know that inside the box, live insects had crawled out of the nest, awaiting further developments.

Wayne's fingers pried open the flaps, and out they shot— not aerial yellow jackets, thank heaven, but plump gray flies, four in number. Thus liberated, the flies buzzed off to the closest window and gathered there. Among them trailed a paper wasp. Fortunately, it was in no temper for stinging.

As you might imagine, all this proved highly entertaining for Wayne's colleagues standing on the sidelines. Lucky for me they were all entomologists.

Knowing there might be more aeronauts where the flies and the wasp came from, Wayne slid the box into one plastic bag, then another, and put it in a freezer. The next day, he retrieved it. This time the cardboard flaps opened and all was still.

The preceding week, Wayne had identified aerial yellow jackets (deceased) I had mailed him from the same nest. So keen was his interest in the species that I decided to give him a look at the nest that had spawned the specimens.

Wayne dove into the papery globe to see what it harbored. Inside, beneath layer after strudel-like layer, he found a several-tiered wedding cake of a comb system in which the hornets had raised their young.

There were corpses, too. A necrology soon arrived in my own mailbox, and I was delighted. Inside the yellow jacket nest Wayne had found the following: six identifiable cluster flies (*Pollenia rudis*), one probable cluster fly mashed under a flap, one paper wasp (very likely *Polistes fuscatus*), three Asian multicolored lady beetles (*Harmonia axyridis*), and fifteen aerial yellow jackets (*Dolichovespula arenaria*), all but one in fine condition.

The story teaches three lessons. First, whenever you send a friend a hornet's nest, seal it inside one or more plastic bags before you take it to the post office.

Second, be careful opening packages sent to you by naturalists.

Third, the builders of a hornet's nest (yellow jackets are well-dressed hornets) may not be the edifice's only users. The flies, wasp, and lady beetles Wayne found inside the nest I sent him had probably crawled into it seeking shelter. Not a bad idea, when you think of it. All those papery layers make for effective insulation, and snug within them, the invaders could hope to ride out a cozy winter.

In the Adirondacks in late autumn, there eventually comes a sobering time when the leaves are gone, the skies are gray, and all the world looks bleak and barren. Mornings grow dark. Evenings shorten, then disappear entirely. No birds sing. Only the cawing of crows punctuates the silence. Grimly black, keen of eye, crows patrol the countryside like teams of undertakers, plucking up the victims of frosts.

Dark thoughts pierce holes in one's equanimity this time of year. The fecundity and generosity of nature, often much on our minds in September and early October as we relish the summer's last fresh tomatoes and autumn's first fresh apples, are nowhere apparent. Turn in any direction and you see death and decay, not beginnings but endings, not life but the bare walls left behind when life leaves the building.

Examine the stage a little more closely, however, and you'll find more than unmitigated tragedy.

Consider, for example, the birds with pale bills that arrive in flocks about the time the last leaves come down. They're sparrows, but perhaps not the kind you're used to. They wear not the brown, streaky camouflage worn by their conventional cousins, but formal wear of charcoal-gray and white. Such sparrows are called juncos. The species we see in the Adirondack Mountains is the dark-eyed. If you want to put a fine point on it, the particular junco we see is a subspecies of the dark-eyed known as the slate-colored.

A flock of juncos provides a happy sight on a cold, gray morning. At once you'll notice the tails, dark in the middle and bordered on each side in white. Then the gray backs catch your eye, and you'll observe that the gray varies in shade. Some birds have backs so dark they look almost black. These are males. Others have light gray backs. These are females.

While picking over a patch of ground for seeds, juncos often keep in touch with each other by uttering gentle tinkling notes and trills. I savor these sounds. In a season woefully short on birdsong, junco voices cheer the ears.

Blunder into a flock of juncos. The birds rise up and flit away, looking like confetti scattered by the wind.

Of course, there's more to cheer about in the second half of autumn than the uniforms of juncos. I find great pleasure in October and November's common scents—the fetid but familiar smell of viburnum leaves, the aroma of wild apples picked and gnawed, the vanilla-like fragrance that hovers over certain places in the woods and whose origin I have never managed to determine.

Winter all but shuts down the human olfactory sense, at least outdoors. But while autumn lingers, opportunities abound for sniffing. I'm not sure why, but a whiff of decaying leaves in November always makes me feel a little more alive.

October comes, then November. Adirondack weather turns persistently cold. I feel an urge to do as many insects do: to cocoon. Of all the strategies devised by the animal kingdom to survive through our hard winters, this one holds the greatest appeal.

Think of it. One day you start feeling sluggish. Your appetite is off, like a monarch butterfly caterpillar preparing to pupate. What do you do?

You find a quiet, sheltered place. Spin yourself a mummy sleeping bag out of silk, or simply rest. In a comfortable position, you wait.

Weeks pass, then months. Snow piles up, then melts. One day in spring or summer, after a long sleep, you stir.

Here comes the exciting part. Unlike the hibernating woodchuck, which rises in spring the same old marmot it was last autumn, you emerge from your chrysalis a new person.

Imagine what it must be like to go to sleep a lowly inchworm and wake up a moth. Or to stiffen like a monarch caterpillar, assume the appearance of a glass Christmas ornament, and burst out a stained-glass-orange butterfly. Adirondack monarchs pass through their pupal stage in summer and spend the winter in tropical forests as adults.

Among butterflies, the tiger swallowtail is probably the best known of those that wait out winter inside chrysalides. Their caterpillars begin existence looking like dribbles of bird excrement, but slowly fatten and lengthen. By the time they start feeling the urge to retreat from the world, tiger swallowtail larvae have turned green or brown and developed a mesmerizing pair of eye-spots.

Then it happens. One day a larva stops feeding on the leaves of, say, a willow, then lashes itself to a twig or some other stable structure. (We have one affixed to a shingle on the side of our house.) Over the course of many days, it stops looking like a caterpillar and commences giving the impression of a Grecian urn.

It must be strange, and not all unpleasant, to disappear inside an enameled vessel as a homely juvenile, later to emerge a glamorous and full-fledged adult. No difficult adolescence for the tiger swallowtail. The journey from childhood to maturity is made in a single dizzying leap.

What then? The swallowtail butterfly is a nectar feeder, but for a great many insects, diet is done away with, and adulthood consists entirely of romance.

No wonder butterflies fascinate poets. Butterflies begin life as tiny, jewel-like eggs, pass through a demanding apprenticeship, retreat from the world inside chrysalides of various forms, then are reborn as creatures of passion—obsessed lovers on wings.

Perhaps we all aspire to re-make ourselves in higher form, and that's why cocooning holds such appeal. Imagine: one dark, cold day you slip into oblivion, only to awaken again in light and warmth, as if no time had passed, a winged being rising toward the sun.

It snows all night and all morning. By noon, when Debbie and I step out into six inches of fluff, the onslaught is lessening. Fine, dust-like flakes sift down on our heads, and the sky brightens.

Just then, Debbie and I happen to look in the same direction. Perhaps movement catches our interest, or maybe it's just a matter of logic—of looking to the row of firs that forms the southerly border of our lawn, and that on days such as this we know will look grand in a fresh coat of snow. I suppose the reason doesn't matter. What does is that we look.

There it is! The apparition is a bird, not one of the chickadees, nuthatches, goldfinches, tree sparrows, and woodpeckers that haunt our feeder these days, but something utterly new. It's as white as the snow, although the wing-tips are dark. The size—big, like a crow—suggests, along with its flap-and-glide style of flight, that it's some kind of hawk.

But what kind? We see few if any hawks this time of year.

The bird shoots through the cold clear air from left to right, nearly invisible at first but growing conspicuous as its altitude drops. The white shape against a white background becomes a white shape against the dark, sheltered nooks created beneath the snow-catching limbs of a balsam fir. Now we can see details: lanky wings, wingtips that are blunt and black, and a relatively long tail.

Strangely, as though this is a performance staged for our benefit, the sun burns through the clouds at just the right instant. A beam shoots through and strikes the bird. It glows.

Debbie, always quick on the draw where birds are concerned, makes the identification. "Marsh hawk," she says, meaning a species labeled "northern harrier" in the latest generation of bird books. "A male."

So it is. During the brief interval between the first glimpse and the moment, two or three seconds later, when the bird dives into the forest, I entertain thoughts of a gyrfalcon, a white raptor of the Arctic that makes rare appearances in our part of the world. Yet this bird's wing-tips are too black and not pointed enough, and its tail is too attenuated. Truth is, it's a marsh hawk.

A marsh hawk! Still, this is a treat. What business has the bird in our yard this wild, wintry late November morning? It ought to be on the coast, or farther south. Yet here it is, airborne, passing through our lives in far less time than it takes to read this sentence, and we, if not necessarily the bird, feel the richer for it.

Between autumn and winter in the Adirondacks lies a sliver of the calendar known as Indian summer. Nearly all the leaves are down, but the snowpack isn't. Days are often balmy, nights bracing. In the woods, coppery beech leaves, which are the last to drop, flutter on pewter twigs. In swamps, tamarack needles, their summer green alchemized to gold, hang suspended between death and decomposition. On breezy days, they fall like dry rain. Warm, muted sunshine slants across the landscape, flattering every object.

Out for a ramble this mild, radiant morning, I notice familiar features of the season-between-seasons. There are goldfinches, impoverished of color after their autumn molt, flitting gaily from treetop to treetop. I hear them before I see them. Weird rising buzzes give the finches away, although at this time of year, when closely related pine siskins begin turning up in droves, I need visual confirmation before I'm certain the bird in the ear is a goldfinch.

Goldfinches breed well into the autumn, taking advantage of the opening of thistle seeds. Perhaps that's why in Indian summer, when other birds are comporting themselves with the high seriousness of school board members, goldfinches still chatter and chase each other like freshmen. For them, the season of love and youth lives on.

I admire slender, finger-like buds adorning the branches of a yellow birch. The birch is both pessimist and optimist. Despite gorgeous weather, it has dropped its leaves, locked away water in safe places between cells, and battened down hatches to prevent winter desiccation. At the same time, the tree avows its faith in next year's spring by waving buds in the sunshine. Inside each of them, a proto-leaf or proto-flower awaits moisture, sugar, and a hormonal messenger to tell it May will soon be coming.

American crows have a good deal to say to each other today, and it's no surprise. Crows have two seasons. At breeding time, they pair off and avoid social contact. As nest raiders, crows tend to look suspiciously on the presence of neighboring crows near their eggs or unfledged offspring. But the eggs hatch and the young birds grow quickly. Soon it's the other season for crows. By day, the birds disperse far and wide to feed, but just before nightfall they reconvene for mass communal slumber parties. Crow roosts tend to be placed in dense evergreens and may hold hundreds of birds.

Circling our house, I find walls and windows barnacled with Asian ladybugs, the nightmarish spawn of an attempt to employ the insects as biological pest control for aphids. The ladybugs eat aphids, all right, but they've flourished so widely that they've become pests themselves, and no solution has been found for restraining them. Asian ladybugs come from all points of the compass to jam themselves into crannies in our eaves and attic. There they endure the long Adirondack winter or escape to rain down on us during a January thaw.

The day is so peaceful, so gentle, that I find it hard to imagine the winter that looms just ahead. But the ice, snow, and cold will come. We've already had a taste of it. The sky will turn gray, the north wind will blow, water will freeze in buckets, and snow will fall and fall until we're digging into closets for insulated boots and snowshoes.

Through the frigid months, when we crave heat, a false white blanket will cast a spell over the landscape, radiating the few crumbs of warmth that fall on us in winter back into outer space. We'll think back fondly then on days like this one, after the leaves and before the snow, when wedges of geese track southward across the autumn sky and the earth still lies soft underfoot.

Winter

The onset of the Adirondack winter always astonishes me with its brutality. One day our world is wet, warm, and leafy, and the next, it seems, Arctic winds gallop in like Visigoths. The slaughter lays waste to an entire landscape.

Grass stems lie strewn across our uncut lawn like fallen soldiers. Trees look as if a thermonuclear device was exploded nearby, stripping gray trunks of foliage and extinguishing all vital signs. Nearly all the birds are gone. Every drop of water has been rendered useless by freezing, and above the snowpack, lethal temperatures conspire with North winds to murder the unwary.

But wait. The cataclysm is partly an illusion. Life still thrives in a thousand places, perhaps most impressively inside the trunks and limbs of trees.

Consider the balsam poplar I planted last year, and that I'm paying a visit to on New Year's morning. It could not look more dead. Out of the snow rises a single stem, gray, leafless, encrusted with a few brown buds. Nothing suggests it is other than a prospective stick of kindling.

Yet the poplar lives, a stoical version of its summer self. Metabolic functions have slowed to a virtual halt, and like an unheated summer house whose pipes have been drained, water within cells has been spirited away to places between cells. There it freezes without piercing holes in delicate membranes. In a process not fully understood, ice forms between the cells of a balsam poplar without developing the usual sharp-pointed crystals.

This is one reason the tree ranks among the most cold-hardy in North America. Without central heating or much in the way of insulation, a balsam poplar can survive temperatures as low as 112 degrees below zero Fahrenheit.

Contrast this with the more fragile constitution, where freezing is concerned, of the tree known as the "live oak." This titan of the American South bursts its bark if temperatures fall below eighteen degrees Fahrenheit. Yet every species has its talents. When a hurricane tears into a Gulf Coast forest, live oaks may be the only trees left standing.

As a rule, Adirondack trees are resilient. When they do freeze, death is not inevitable. Walk through the woods here and you'll find trunks split by frost but still very much alive. Bark and sapwood crack open when trees face temperatures colder than they can bear.

What about evergreens? They hang on to their leaves in winter, but for the most part they, too, winterize themselves to the point where metabolic processes slow to a near-halt. Photosynthesis takes place rarely, if at all, even on warm bright days.

But, alive Adirondack evergreens certainly are. They look inert, but the necessary engines of life chug along at an idle. Then spring comes. The ground thaws, water in the soil melts, and sugar factories in evergreen leaves are up and running at a time when the solar-powered cells of those late sleepers, the deciduous trees, are just beginning to stir.

This morning, I step outside into the Ice Age. According to the radio, the temperature measures twenty-one degrees below zero. According to the thermometer on our porch, the temperature hangs at six below. I chose to believe the radio. Later on, it'll make for a better story.

So there I am, braving the elemental elements, when from out of the woods and into my ears comes a voice of cheer: the high, tinkling notes of a brown creeper, singing as if it were April.

How now? Surely, the bird effuses under no misapprehension that it's time to hunt for a girlfriend. Any female brown creeper in her right mind is tucked in an evergreen tree somewhere, or cuddled inside a curl of bark, not out squandering energy she'll have to replace one frozen insect at a time.

But one never knows. Birds are fickle, particularly here. Great-horned owls court on freezing midwinter nights, filling the darkness with their soft but insistent hoots. And I've stood with my feet in the snow, shivering, looking skyward, watching a red-tailed hawk male match aerobatic circles, carefully, with a much larger and potentially lethal female. She's bigger and more powerful than he is and could cut short the courtship at any time with a single swipe of muscle-bound leg and talons.

Last week, on another frosty morning, the chickadees that haunt our bird feeder sang in counterpoint. I hadn't heard a plaintive *Dee-dee* in months. Yet there they were, half notes in four-four time. What inspired them? Chickadees won't sing with any frequency until March. Perhaps it was the morning sunshine. That glow inspired me, too.

Whenever in winter I find myself surprised and delighted

by a sound, I'm reminded of the night, about twenty years ago, when I was walking alone in the woods and heard the music of fairies.

Winter had just arrived. I was skirting the shore of a lake, cold but not yet frozen. I stopped to listen for animal sounds and was astounded to hear the tinkling of tiny bells.

The source was very near. But where? I cupped my ears, turned left, turned right, and spun around. The sound grew loudest in volume when I turned northward–the direction of the lake. I aimed my ears high, then low. The sound came from my feet.

I got down on all-fours. Doing everything but wagging my tail, I nosed around like a dog. No doubt about it: the magical elfin notes rose straight from the water.

A thoroughbred romantic would have left it right there, turned away, and brought home a mystery. But I have a left brain as well as a right brain, and the left cried for science. I switched on a flashlight.

No fairies danced into view. But there, gliding like yachts across the lake's glossy surface, appeared ice crystals, or aggregations of crystals, several inches long, flat, and pointed like daggers. A slight breeze stirred them. As ice struck ice, music drifted into the night. No one was there to see, but I know I smiled until my face hurt.

The symphony of a freezing pond and the singing of brown creepers and black-capped chickadees in January have this much in common. They leave a feeling that life, whatever its traumas, is going to provide you abundant surprises. The feeling feels good.

After you've been keeping an eye on birds for a while, you start to get antsy. You've identified all the sparrows and wood-warblers in the neighborhood, and when a rusty blackbird turns up among the red-wings or a white-crowned sparrow slips in with the white-throats, you're hardly surprised. Perhaps you've seen it all. Or have you?

The good naturalist knows there's always more to discover—birds that defy the range maps and flit in from afar, birds with unfamiliar plumages, albino birds, partial albinos, birds that belt out songs different from those they're supposed to sing, and familiar birds that behave in ways that surprise you. Keep your eyes peeled and ears clear.

For me, it's a particular pleasure to see a bird I think I know well doing something I've never seen it do before. For example, cedar waxwings were old hat to me, or so I thought, until a day when I came upon them making a nest. The interesting thing wasn't that the waxwings were weaving plant fibers into a cup. It was that the birds were taking the materials from an oriole's nest, which itself was under construction.

The waxwings were cagey. They'd wait for the female oriole to return with a mouthful of fibers and tuck them into the hanging basket she was fashioning. Then, when the oriole flew off, the waxwings would move in, dismantle, and steal.

Now it's early winter. The prospects for catching birds making nests are poor. This morning I go for a walk, expecting to see nothing extraordinary and ending up making a discovery.

Old hands at bird-watching will read these words and laugh at my naiveté. But I confess that until this day, I had never witnessed birds eating snow.

This is what I see. I stroll down the road, bundled up like an astronaut against a subzero Adirondack chill, looking here and there for signs of animal life, when the movement of several birds in the top of an evergreen tree catches my eye.

The distance is great, and the birds look tiny. At first, I take them for common redpolls or pine siskins. But binoculars prove otherwise. They're purple finches—common apparitions here during the warm months, but birds I rarely see in winter. A female purple finch looks like a boldly streaked sparrow. A male, it has been famously said, looks like a sparrow dipped in strawberry juice.

As I stand gawking, two of the females fly toward me and land overhead. No sooner have I begun to admire their handsome striped faces than both birds commence gorging on snow that forms a fringe along the twigs. I'm certain of what I see.

At first doubting my own conclusion, I watch to make sure the birds aren't chopping through the snow to get at buds or seeds. But there is no mistake: the finches happily munch the snow itself, and I see their beaks and tongues tackling the job in concert.

Walking home, I think about the fact that Adirondack birds go through long spells when no water in liquid form is available to them. It makes sense that they turn to snow as a substitute, even though melting the snow in their crops or stomachs puts extra demands on their central heating systems. But having never seen the behavior with my own eyes or found the behavior described in print, I thank serendipity for the lesson.

All my life I've craved a good look at a bobcat. In thirty years of searching, from Maine to Florida and Wyoming to Texas, I've glimpsed the elusive, beagle-sized, night-stalking prowler only twice. Both sightings lasted milliseconds. They were so fleeting that I'm left wondering how much I really saw and how much I imagined.

On various occasions, I've identified bobcat footprints in Adirondack snow. But then, I've never considered myself an expert tracker, so doubt clouds those sightings, too.

This week, everything changes.

Late in the afternoon, I'm editing an essay-in-progress in an outbuilding when Debbie shouts to me over an intercom. "Ed, there's a cat on the ground near the bird feeder. I think it's a bobcat!" Any naturalist who knows Debbie listens closely when she gets excited. Eyes don't come any sharper and she knows an unusual animal when she sees one.

From my studio, the only way I can hope to get a look at the prospective bobcat is to climb partway up a wall, pull open a window, and let bone-numbing winter air pour into my cozy space. I look in the direction of the bird feeder. Something brown seems to be crouched there, but at a distance of a couple of hundred feet, I can't see detail. Hoping to get the animal to look up and give me a glimpse of its face, I hoot like an owl. This works, but I'm still uncertain. I try to convince myself I'm seeing a bobcat, but in the gray light of late afternoon, with no binoculars at hand, the best I can say is "maybe."

Meanwhile Debbie, locking the intercom in broadcast mode, positions herself in front of the kitchen window. The glass looks straight out on the—on whatever it is. Our son, Ned, two-and-a-half years old, joins her.

Debbie relays the pertinent details. The thing is definitely a cat, but it seems too large to be a housecat. It's golden brown all over, except the face, from which radiate dark stripes. The ears are big and pointed at the tips. The fur looks wonderfully thick and woolly.

Trapped in the studio, where a creak of the door will almost certainly scare the cat away, I groan in frustration. "Deb, the tail, the tail, what about the tail?" In the kitchen, Debbie's intercom transmits continuously, and she can't hear me. It's just as well. The animal's crouch blocks her view of the tail we both desperately want to see.

Debbie grows more and more excited. So does Ned. "Dada, a bobcat!" he says at least six times. By this time, Dada feels sorry for himself. At two-and-a-half, Ned enjoys a view of a bobcat far superior to anything his father has seen in his nearly fifty years.

When Debbie tells me she's had her fill, I step out the door. I take pains to advance silently, but the snow on this frigid winter day crunches like peanut shells. I reach the bird feeder. Nothing's there. Debbie tells me later that the cat lingered until I was a few feet away. A car and snowbank blocked my view until it was too late.

The bobcat sauntered away, she said, apparently confident in its ability to vanish among the trees. When it stood up, Debbie and Ned saw the naturally abbreviated tail, which gives the bobcat its name.

Luckily for me, that isn't the end of it. The following morning, I put out fresh sardines, sardines perhaps having lured the cat to appear in the first place. (I put fish out every week or two to encourage visits from an ermine.) Hardly have I returned to the kitchen than Debbie blurts something unintelligible from the bedroom.

I don't have to ask. Her excitement can mean only one thing. Hurrying to the kitchen window, my electrified eyeballs gaze upon a bobcat. It stands on four delicate cat feet, just beyond the glass, padding slowly and confidently along a path between the woodshed and the kitchen door. It's my good luck that a few drops of sardine oil dripped on the ground directly beneath the window. For twenty or thirty delicious seconds, the bobcat pauses to sniff. I take it all in—the definitive field marks Debbie described yesterday over the intercom, right down to the animal's short, furry sausage of a tail.

For five minutes, we keep the cat in view. It passes the feeder, struts up a path to the driveway, and strikes off across the lawn. When it disappears, we run to the porch on the far side of the house. The bobcat pays no attention to us. It reaches the road we live on, walks along it a hundred feet or so, ambles across a one-lane-bridge, and descends to an ice-covered river. Keeping to the riverbank it pads downstream. With binoculars, we follow it for a quarter mile. I stand in the cold in my pajamas, shivering from sheer joy.

Perhaps, like me, you've wondered where the animals in your neck of the woods hibernate. I don't mean the general locations. I mean the specific spots, say, that a jumping mouse snoozes the winter away beneath the red maple at the top of the driveway, six feet east of the trunk and thirty-eight inches down. Wouldn't it be exciting to look around with X-ray glasses and see through the snow and frozen earth to all the places where overwintering creatures are sleeping?

As a kid, I bought a pair of X-ray glasses from the Johnson Smith novelty catalog. I knew they wouldn't work, but I was curious to know what, if anything, the glasses could really do. The answer came swiftly: they could do nothing.

So I spent the next few decades similarly in the dark, musing about the locations of hibernating animals, until one April evening a couple of years ago. It was dusk. Debbie and I were strolling up our long driveway, which is walled in on both sides by hydrangea bushes. We heard a strange rustling.

Cupping our ears and swiveling this way and that, we determined that the sounds came from the leaf litter under the hydrangeas on the driveway's north shoulder. We looked closely and could see places where leaves trembled. In a Stephen King novel, this is the point at which zombies would erupt from the ground, spewing evil.

But zombies and evil were nowhere to be seen. In one of the places where the leaves stirred with particular enthusiasm, a face popped out. We recognized it at once as belonging to an American toad.

One plump, warty toad after another wriggled into view until darkness and mosquitoes chased us home. Debbie and I were both exhilarated. We see toads nearly every warm day where we live, but to witness a veritable herd of them bursting simultaneously from hibernacula in our own backyard was almost too much excitement for pair of naturalists to bear.

Today, with the temperature climbing to around twenty degrees Fahrenheit and deep snow blanketing the ground, I think of those toads, perhaps tucked back in the same places, alive, somnolent, hearts beating occasionally, blood oozing through their plumbing at a lazy pace, yet ready, if conditions demand it, to dig.

American toads possess nothing like the superb frost-protection of wood frogs, which in winter permeate their tissues with anti-freeze. Toads die if their body temperatures drop much below freezing. To survive the winter, they must bury themselves where frost cannot find them.

The burying is done with sweeping jabs of the back legs. Leaf litter and soil are pushed aside, and the toads back into the resulting parking spaces. The depth to which the diggers descend probably varies from place to place as well as week to week. Studies of a closely related amphibian in Manitoba showed that as winter progresses and the frost penetrates ever deeper into the soil, the toads keep descending, too, staying just out of reach of the frost.

Today, snow lies all about, deep and crisp and even. I ponder the toads that sleep beneath it, each snug inside a form-fitting hibernaculum. My own busy life contrasts sharply with that of a wintering toad, and I find myself thinking that it wouldn't be bad to close one's eyes in October, open them again in April, and wake up rested and refreshed amid the first blush of spring.

Beautiful fresh snow turns to old cold slush, and a gray sky spits rain. June in January? Global warming? My mood could be cheerier this morning when, chained to my desk and in the middle of a long writing project, I catch a glimpse of a bird.

It's tiny, too tiny to be a chickadee. What then? Perhaps a kinglet. I leap from my chair, surprised by my own enthusiasm, and bolt for an east-facing window.

I find a scene right out of a Japanese painting. The twisting limbs and twigs of a wild black cherry tree loom starkly against parchment-white snow. In the middle of the scene, an artist's template of a bird clings, its body as round as a golf ball, a small head and bill sketched on the left side of the circle, a tail tagged on the right.

A kinglet? Perhaps. Smaller than the average warbler? Yes. Olive-green with delicate white bars across the wings? Check. Possessed of a delicate, tweezers-like bill? Indeed. Features support the theory.

OK, it's a kinglet. But which kind? There are two. Ruby-crowned kinglets turn up in our corner of the Adirondacks in springtime and sing their brassy songs through most of the summer, but we generally say good-bye to them in autumn. At this time of year, any kinglet seen is likely to be a golden-crowned.

Of course, because the kinglet is all but certain to be a golden-crowned, that doesn't mean it actually is one. Ruby-crowns turn up occasionally. I'd better have a look.

The dreary light is far from ideal for spotting subtleties, so I brace for failure. Yet no sooner do I look for a dark streak through the eye, a white eyebrow, and a golden crown than the drab little bird turns and displays all of them for me.

What's the kinglet doing? In winter, a tiny bird must feed from break of day to dusk in order to keep its metabolism stoked, so I'm not surprised to find this one gleaning. "Glean" is an S.A.T. word rarely included in the modern American vernacular, at least until you become a birdwatcher. Then you watch gleaning, hear talk of gleaning, and glean knowledge of gleaning every time you and your binocular-toting friends run into kinglets.

To glean is to skim the surface of things, grabbing whatever turns up. Brown creepers mostly specialize in gleaning bugs and spiders from tree trunks. Kinglets take on the branches and twigs. A difference between the two kinglet species is that golden-crowns frequently dangle upside down, picking at the undersides of twigs, while ruby-crowns generally work the upsides.

What is the golden-crowned kinglet finding to eat? The naturalist Bernd Heinrich gives some idea in his excellent *Winter World: The Ingenuity of Animal Survival* (Harper Collins, 2003). Heinrich examined the stomach contents of a golden-crown and found it contained not springtails, which the scientific literature suggested were its principal winter food source, but thirty-nine tiny inchworms.

Inchworms are the larvae of geometrid moths. The foremost geometrid expert in the world couldn't identify the larvae, so Heinrich collected live caterpillars and reared them. The experiment failed at first, but repeated attempts eventually solved the mystery. The kinglets were feeding largely on the rice-grain-size larvae of *Hypagyrtis unipunctata*, a drab moth sometimes called the one-spotted variant.

So that's what my kinglet is up to! As I stand in a warm office, looking through glass, the little entomologist, wrapped in warm feathers, works its way through the cherry tree, gathering up its day's pay while I go back to earning mine.

It's a cold, snowy Adirondack morning, the temperature below zero and not going to rise anytime soon. We nose the car down the driveway, heading for the mailbox and beyond. Half asleep, we're barely paying attention to what's ahead when Debbie and I notice three strange birds on the driveway.

The birds, a little more compact than robins, appear strange because their profiles don't quite add up to any we usually see this time of year. The tails are long, but not as long as blue jay tails. The heads look handsomely round, without crests, and the bellies are plump. As for the bills, they're short, sturdy, and nearly round.

Suddenly the sun brightens. Our windshield clears, and our brains begin to make sense of the signals streaming from our eyes. The birds are fanned out left to right, and I make out the right-hand one's colors. They're out of the ordinary. The head is rusty, the back, belly, and flanks gray, the wings and tail black. Each wing wears a pair of corporal's stripes, white as new snow.

Before I can think, and before either of us gets a good look at the second and third birds, all three lift off the ground. They swirl toward the sky and are gone, yet not for long. As we near the bottom of the drive, Debbie spies one of the group in a tamarack tree on the far side of the road.

It's the bird I had a look at, the one with the rusty head. We fumble for binoculars. The object of our interest is forgiving. It's still perched about a foot from the trunk, halfway up the tree, when we bring it into ten-power view.

By this time we're both pretty certain we know the apparition's identity. It's a pine grosbeak. We haven't seen one in years. Later in the day, looking in David Sibley's thorough and up-to-date field guide, we learn that the rusty-headed bird is a female or an immature male.

Where you find one pine grosbeak, you're apt to find a flock. Experts lump these birds with red-winged crossbills, white-winged crossbills, and a few other species as "irruptive winter finches." If you stay home, you'll go years without seeing them, until the cone crops fail up North. (In a typical year, the great conifer forests due north of the Adirondacks in Canada produce spruce, fir, pine, and tamarack cones in staggering abundance. But from time to time, and sometimes all at once across a spectrum of species, cone numbers crash.) Then winter finches appear everywhere, in blizzards of feathers. Sometimes the birds are so tame that housecats slaughter piles of them and human admirers come near stepping on them when they feed on the ground.

We look for the two that got away. Almost instantly I find them, perched within inches of each other in the top of an adjacent tree. They're showcased in strong light, and we can't restrain ourselves from oohing and ahhing. These are males. Their colors dazzle. A luminous pinkish red covers most of each bird, with black wings, bold white wingbars, and what might be called gray undershorts.

For a moment, I try to turn the birds into white-winged crossbills, which are similarly marked. But Debbie reminds me why they're not. The tails are too long, their size too large, the signature overbite and underbite of crossbills nowhere to be seen.

As we gawk, tamarack scales flutter to the ground. The birds are feeding. Will they linger? Not a chance. Instantly, as if cued to do so, all three drop, beat their strong wings, and zoom out of view. That's how these birds behave. Meanwhile, we're left to wonder. Will we see a hundred more by the end of the day, or must we wait years to glimpse the next one?

Here in the Adirondacks, you never know when you'll run into colorful characters.

Sunday, Debbie, our son Ned, and I go for a drive. The initial purpose is to cross the county to a place where Bohemian waxwings have been seen. These are birds of Canada and the high Rockies that wander south and east in winter, occasionally turning up in New York and New England. I've chased birds on both sides of the Equator for twenty-five years and never managed to see one.

On this particular day, I can't stop thinking about a magazine article I wrote a week earlier. In it I'd criticized the recklessness with which we—you, me, our civilization in general—consume fossil fuels that took millions of years to accumulate. Yet here we are, driving miles and miles in an automobile for the frivolous purpose of trying to see a bird. I gag on my own hypocrisy.

A few miles from our driveway, guilt gets the better of us, and we trade our initial plan for a better one. We'll forget about the waxwings, loop home by way of a country road we haven't traveled before, and take an environmentally responsible stroll from our doorstep.

Just past a lake and a place where picnic tables poke through the snow, I veer left on a narrow road. It leads up and up, then down and down, eventually bottoming out in a low place flooded by beavers.

Trees that didn't appreciate the work of the Rodent Corps of Engineers stand dead, bleached, and stripped of all but their stoutest branches. Debbie and I scan them. We know that dead trees attract birds like cheese lures mice. We see nothing— nothing, that is, until the wetland begins to slip away behind us. Then, out of the corner of my left eye, I glimpse a dozen or so dark, starling-sized shapes clustered in a pair of trees.

Birds? Perhaps. Either that or dead pine cones. To learn the answer, I throw the car into reverse. Before we've come to a stop Debbie and I both see that the two trees are filled with sleek gray-brown songbirds. They're distinguished by slicked-back crests on their heads and stark black faces.

Waxwings. Fifteen of them, to be exact. I see at once that these are bigger and grayer than the cedar waxwings common in the Adirondacks in the warm months. They wear their field marks like jewelry and make-up: a flash of ruby at the tips of the secondary feathers, two daubs of white on the wing, a golden thunderbolt shooting toward the wingtip, mascara applied boldly around the eyes and mouth, and a band of yellow spanning the outer reach of the tail.

Sometimes when I see a new bird, aside from the fact that I've never seen it before, it's hardly worth raising binoculars or an eyebrow. But these Bohemians merit a "Yahoo!" They're gorgeous.

Home we drive, virtue not completely forsaken and the bird, so to speak, in the hand.

I'm out for a solo hike, bushwhacking down the spine of a geologic formation that interests me, when I turn to look back on my tracks and notice a dark object far off in the northern sky. I haven't seen a bird all day, and in the woods, I've heard only a few black-capped chickadees and a red-breasted nuthatch. Distance reduces the approaching flier to a speck, but somehow I know at once it's an eagle.

Binoculars give the vision shape. I see no color, but the outline and proportions are clear: a head without much of a neck, long broad wings that appear to end in fingers, and a wide fanned tail, blunt like a crow's. There's something about an eagle's wings that give the bird away. I suppose it's the extraordinary length of the wings relative to the size of the bird's torso. Just as a gorilla is built on the human body plan, except for proportionately longer arms useful for brachiating, the eagle in flight resembles a large hawk, only its wings are distinctly longer.

I hope the eagle will come close, either for a look at me, or simply because it's tracking overhead. The dark shape grows larger and larger until it passes directly above my head. I crane my neck and gaze up at the bird's gorilla-wings, and at the powerful torso that might have been shaded with charcoal pencil. The head and tail appear as emphatically white as the snow heaped up at my feet.

The eagle scrutinizes me with yellow eyes. I admire it with green. I can't put my finger on why eye contact with a wild animal gives me a thrill, yet it always does. One of the highlights for me of a year spent hobnobbing with wildlife in Australia and New Zealand was a morning in Eungella National Park in Queensland, when, at first light, I crouched beside a river watching duck-billed platypuses dive for crayfish. One of the bizarre egg-laying mammals bobbed up in front of me and drilled me straight in the eye. I gasped for sheer delight. I'd seen Australia, and now Australia had had a look at me.

Seeing, and being seen: it's an age-old game. Play it with a grizzly bear out West, or with a tiger in the wilds of India or Siberia, and you may come out the loser. Yet where I live in the Adirondack Mountains of eastern North America, the sport is as safe as croquet or horseshoes. From my viewpoint, it's also considerably more fun.

If you want to approach an animal closely, making eye contact with it is not a particularly good idea. This is why photographers, me among them, are forever employing what's called the "lost wallet trick." As you move nearer and nearer to an animal, you stare at the ground and scan back and forth, as if looking for a lost wallet or contact lens. Your disinterest reassures the beast. The ruse works wonderfully well.

If, on the other hand, you're in a Zen frame of mine, enthralled with the moment and pleased to accept things as they are, try this. Fix your eyes on your subject's and relish the ensuing meeting of souls. That's what I do here. The eagle can no more imagine itself in my shoes than I can fully imagine myself in its feathers, drifting across a winter sky. But that's the pleasure. The raptor, in its unfathomable way, looks down in wonder on what it sees, and I gaze up and savor our differentness and my place in nature's sprawling democracy of species.

The newest word in my two-year-old son's rapidly expanding vocabulary is "frisky." Ned frisks around the house and the yard like only a toddler can, so it seemed high time I introduce him to the word. He added it to his repertoire at once—just in the nick of time, as it happened, to share in our first sighting on home turf of a wild animal for whom the word might well have been coined.

Debbie, cradling Ned's baby sister, Tasman, in her arms, spies the oversized, aquatic weasel from a bedroom window. "Hurry," she shouts to the male half of the household. Ned and I are slouching on the living room couch. "There's something down by the river I know you'll want to see."

Ned and I waste no time. Sprinting for the bedroom and the window, I hold Ned to the glass and we both look out on his mother's discovery: a sleek, dark brown, densely furred embodiment of friskiness, sausage-shaped like its weasel cousins, but with a mass comparable to that of a full-sized dachshund. It's a river otter.

A couple of hundred yards of snow-covered ground, black water, and ice stretch between the otter and us. Even without binoculars, we enjoy a satisfying look at its peculiar shape and gait. The distinctive otter snout, blunt and rounded like the business end of a shovel, sports extravagant whiskers. From the other end projects the trademark otter tail—stout at the base, thickly furred, and tapering to a sword-like point.

What is the animal doing? Being an otter, it humps along awkwardly yet efficiently without a trace of self-consciousness. It's crossing an ice shelf attached to the river's north bank. By afternoon, the ice will be gone, ripped away by the violent current of a river engorged with snowmelt. But this morning, the stark white of the snow-covered ice provides the perfect background to make a dark shape stand out.

The otter gambols over to the edge of the cold, black water, sniffs, and bounds a few feet downstream. Perhaps it's seeking the right diving board. "Look, Ned!" I say, pointing. Ned looks up, and after looking puzzled for a moment, he sees. "An otter!" I tell him. Then, unable to resist reinforcing a recent language lesson, I add, "Frisky!"

A smile breaks across Ned's two-year-old face, and his blue eyes seem to laugh. "Frisky!" he says. "I see an otter. It's frisky!"

Eight-month-old Tassie, more excited by the excitement in the room than the spectacle on the ice, laughs heartily, sharing in the fun.

There's something magnetic about otters. Once years ago, during a behind-the-scenes tour of a private zoo, I had the chance to pet and play with a live one. I count the experience one of the great thrills of my life. The otter, the very picture of friskiness, rollicked around me like a bouncing ball. It darted in and out, nudging me repeatedly and teasingly with its handsome snout. I ran my hand down the slick, felt-like fur of the otter's back and thought I'd never felt anything so marvelous.

Otters are famous for playing hard, especially for making slides in mud or snow and then rocketing down them on their bellies. If he had the chance to join a band of otters, Ned, a connoisseur of slides, would fit right in. Otters work hard, too, diving and swimming speedily through the water in pursuit of fish, frogs, crayfish, birds, eggs of various sorts, and turtles. Some people look so sad you know they've taken up the wrong career, but an otter always appears happy on the job.

The animal we see this morning appears to be at work. It finds a spot along the edge of the ice to its liking, pauses for a moment (as you or I might before jumping into cold water), and plunges. From a bedroom window, we watch for several minutes to see the dark form surface, but the swim must be a long one. The otter comes up for its next breath somewhere out of view.

"Frisky," Ned says as we leave the otter to find its breakfast and head to the kitchen for ours.

The first time I see an ermine at our house, it steals in through an open door and scoots around the baseboards in the kitchen. It's drawn by the scent of a kippered herring sandwich I'm assembling on the counter. The compact but powerful predator, also known as the short-tailed weasel, seems to pour rather than run, its long, cylindrical body a marvel of fluidity. A lustrous chestnut brown colors the back, and I catch a glimpse of a milk-white underside as around and around it goes.

The second time I see an ermine at our house, the kitchen door is firmly shut, and snow lies deep on the ground. I've set out a picked-over chicken carcass to feed a visiting northern shrike, which is a kind of predatory songbird. When I spy the ermine, its dangling by its teeth and swinging like a pendulum, trying to haul the carcass from an elevated bird feeding platform down to the ground. All the chestnut hair is gone. It looks as if someone has dunked the animal in white paint. The only parts that aren't white are black: the tip of the nose and the last inch of the tail.

In the Adirondacks, ermines aren't the only mammals to trade brown for white as winter approaches. Long-tailed weasels do it, too, and so do snowshoe hares. The reason seems obvious. Through a long northern winter, white fur makes for excellent camouflage in snow while brown fur does not.

What seems obvious, however, is not always true. Scientists studying the thermodynamics of animals in winter bring us the startling news that the white fur and white feathers that cover assorted northern mammals and birds in winter may have less to do with camouflage than with keeping their bearers warm.

Why is white warmer than brown? The answer lies in the structure of hair and in the fine divisions, called barbules, that make up feathers. Colored hair and feathers contain a pigment known as melanin. Remove it, and you not only turn the animal white, but you create empty space within its hair filaments or barbules. Such air space acts as insulation. Hollow hair and feathers keep those who possess them warm.

No Adirondack bird turns white in winter, but to the north, around Hudson Bay and beyond, rock and willow ptarmigans (chicken-like birds related to Adirondack ruffed grouse and spruce grouse) molt scalloped-brown plumages at summer's end and replace them with toasty white.

Given the thermal advantages of turning white in winter, it's a wonder more animals here don't do it. But then, perhaps the adaptation is not a matter of black and white. White-tailed deer don't bleach blond in autumn, but they do trade in fine, cinnamon-colored summer coats for coarse gray winter coats. The gray hairs are much less pigmented than the summer ones, and they're thick and hollow. The deer meets the ermine and the hare halfway.

Whether white winter pelage and plumage evolved for reasons of warmth or camouflage may never be known. Perhaps a bit of both was involved. Natural selection, the engine that drives evolution, likely confers a survival advantage on both counts. He or she who stays warm and keeps out of the jaws of predators may endure to see the spring and raise a family.

Back in the dark ages before I wire a pair of spotlights to light up our woodshed after dark, heating our house requires a dangerous fifty-foot trip or two every night, often in pitch blackness, between the kitchen door and the woodpile. "Trip or two" carries double meaning. It's not easy holding a flashlight while simultaneously staggering under an armload of hardwood. The lighting usually suffers, and so, especially when ice covers the ground, does the hindquarters.

One memorable night late in winter, I rouse myself about midnight, put down the book I'm reading, and shuffle outside to retrieve the woodstove's last serving of cordwood. I'm about to step into the impenetrably dark shed when I hear something move. It's only a rustle, so without fear I take another step. Something in the shed hisses at alarming volume.

I'm groggy at midnight, but not foolish. Retreating swiftly to the house, I grab a handheld spotlight and return. This time, the thing hisses again before I get close. I switch on the light. What I see makes me laugh out loud.

Opportunities like this don't come often, so I hurry back to retrieve my naturalist wife. I know she'll be as interested and amused by the intruder as I am. All I tell her is that something hissed at me in the woodshed, and she might want to have a look. When she hesitates, I promise the mysterious visitor won't attack.

Debbie pads out in her slippers while I linger in the lighted kitchen. Seconds later, I hear a whoop. She bursts back in, smiling. "What on earth is a mallard duck doing in our woodshed?" It's a question for which I have no answer.

The river that flows past our house is still frozen, or so we believe. But it's later winter, and perhaps a pool has opened upstream or downstream, hidden from view, and it's caught the duck's attention. In late winter, the first breaks in the river ice expose black water that shouts to ducks passing high overhead. "Stop here for food and romance!" The birds drop down to investigate, and as a result, we get early looks at mallards, hooded mergansers, and wood ducks. Perhaps this mallard drake swooped down late this afternoon, got caught out after dark, and waddled to our shed seeking shelter.

Then again, maybe the bird has another motive. Mallards eat aquatic plants for the most part, although they're not averse to snails, mussels, insect nymphs, tadpoles, and fish. In farm country, mallards sometimes drop into stubble and root around for seeds. Debbie and I aren't farmers, but we do lay out sunflower seed all winter to feed songbirds. It's possible the mallard has come to dine and takes up lodging here as an afterthought.

Either way, the duck is welcome to stay. We look for it the next night and the next, but without success. Just as we begin to get laughs out of friends with our side of the story, perhaps the mallard drifts on a pond somewhere, quacking out a tale to its neighbors of a dark night, a promising shelter, and rude awakening.

Driving home with two kids sleeping soundly in the back seat of the car, I'm tempted to pull over and take a nap myself. I'm exhausted. Yet just as the idea comes to mind, I notice a dark shape in the sky, straight ahead. It's a bird, an unusually large bird, and a second look shows it has two similarly oversized companions.

Bald eagles? Thirty years ago, when I first started taking an active interest in birds, the thought would never have occurred to me. Eagles were scarce. People saw them in Florida and Alaska but as far as I knew rarely anyplace else.

Most of us know why. The pesticide DDT, used to drench the American landscape in the 1950s and 1960s in an attempt to bring mosquitoes and other insect pests to heel, caused the ornithological symbol of the United States to lay thin-shelled eggs. When prospective mothers sat on their eggs to incubate them, the frail things crumbled, destroying the embryos developing inside.

Reproducing slowly or not at all, eagles declined or vanished altogether. The same fate befell peregrine falcons, and to a lesser degree ospreys. All three species might be extinct had not a celebrated nature writer named Rachel Carson sounded the alarm. The pesticide industry and its friends in government counterattacked, but time and science proved Carson right. DDT was banned. Later, efforts were made in various quarters to bring the birds back.

Where I live, those efforts have succeeded, at least where eagles are concerned. The three eagles I see through the windshield represent a rapidly expanding population in the Northeast.

Eagles are seen in our neighborhood mainly in spring, summer, and fall, although this mild winter, the river that passes our house remained open enough to keep the big birds from ever leaving. We see one from time to time, perched stoically in a tree or cruising low over the water.

There's a dam downstream from where we live, and eagles frequent the tall pines just below it. They wait for turbulence to bring fish to the surface, then swoop down and grab. Fishermen also interest the birds. These days, people often throw back more fish than they keep, and many fishermen keep no fish at all. That's all right with the eagles. Fish tossed back make easy pickings.

Through the winter and early spring, our local birds keep an eye on ice fishermen. Bald eagles are to a large degree scavengers, a fact that troubled Benjamin Franklin—who favored the turkey as our national bird—but not the rest of our country's founders. Ice fishermen often store their catch over the course of a day in shallow wells chipped or drilled into the ice. They also refresh their baitfish from time to time, discarding tired and moribund minnows near their holes. Crafty eagles study our habits. When a fisherman walks away, a big bird sometimes drops in to take advantage.

I pull the car over, not to sleep but to watch. Fortunately, I have binoculars. Magnification confirms that all three birds are adult eagles with white heads and white tails. I'm not sure, but one seems considerably larger than the other two. I'm likely seeing a female bird being courted by a pair of smaller males.

My impression that romance is in the air is confirmed by an elegant aerial dance. The birds circle in synchrony, practically brushing wingtips as they trace interlocking circles a hundred feet above the treetops. A gusting west wind quickly blows the eagles out of view, but I don't mind. Debbie and I have two kids to raise, and the birds leave me feeling hopeful.

About the Author

Author, naturalist, and photographer Edward Kanze is a 1978 graduate of Middlebury College, Vermont. He earned a B.A. in Geography and won the Bermas Prize for highest departmental honors. In April 2005, the John Burroughs Association named Ed's essay about the passenger pigeon, *In Search of Something Lost*, as the Outstanding Published Natural History Essay of 2004. The Burroughs awards, bestowed annually at the American Museum of Natural History in New York, are America's highest honors in nature writing. The same essay earned a gold medal in environmental writing by the International Regional Magazine Association.

Ed has published four books:

Kangaroo Dreaming: An Australian Wildlife Odyssey (Random House/Sierra Club, 2000), describes a 25,000-mile journey Ed and Debbie Kanze made among the wild places and wildlife of Australia. Bill McKibben called the book "a superb chronicle of the nature of Australia in all the meanings of that word. You won't be able to read it without wanting to call your travel agent."

The World of John Burroughs (Random House/Sierra Club, paperback 1999; Harry Abrams, hardcover, 1993) portrays the naturalist, philosopher, and literary critic John Burroughs, who lived from 1837-1921. Ed produced the book's seventy color photographs as well as its widely praised text. The late Dean Amadon, Curator Emeritus of Ornithology at the American Museum of Natural History, wrote of the book, "Mr. Kanze writes with a graceful style that would have pleased his subject….Let us hope this volume has the wide circulation it so richly deserves."

Wild Life: The Remarkable Lives of Ordinary Animals (Crown, 1995) collects fifty essays from Ed's syndicated newspaper column. "Anyone with an interest in nature and a sense of humor will love *Wild Life*," says the New Orleans *Times-Picayune*. "Kanze speaks with several voices: that of the professional naturalist full of accurate information and scientific observations; the skilled writer with a grand sense of humor; the storyteller with a sense of drama; and the adult who has the capacity to view the world through the eyes of the curious child."

Notes From New Zealand (Henry Holt, hardcover 1992; paperback, 1993) tells of flightless birds, elusive primitive frogs, and three university-sponsored expeditions to study the tuatara, a superficially lizard-like reptile little changed from creatures that roamed the world's continents before and during the Age of Dinosaurs. "Kanze writes with humor, attention to biological detail, and a love for nature that is contagious," says *The Virginian Pilot*.

"All Things Natural," Ed's weekly newspaper column, has been published since 1987. Today it appears in nine Connecticut and New York newspapers. To date, he has written nearly 1,000 columns. Ed's essays and magazine features have appeared in *Adirondack Life*, *Audubon*, *Birder's*

World, Bird Watcher's Digest, The Conservationist, Garden, Lake Life, Living Bird, Middlebury, National Parks, Reckon, Utne Reader, Vassar Quarterly, and *Wildlife Conservation.* He is a contributing editor at *Bird Watcher's Digest* and writes "The Wild Side" for each issue of *Adirondack Explorer.*

A naturalist and proprietor of the Adirondack Naturalist Company, a licensed Adirondack guiding service, Ed has served as a ranger and writer for the National Park Service in Maine, Florida, Mississippi, and South Dakota; as a field instructor for National Audubon Society ecology workshops; as Senior Naturalist at Teatown Lake Reservation in Ossining, New York; and as Curator of the Trailside Nature Museum in Cross River, New York. A much-published photographer, he shoots for DPA, a natural history stock agency, does freelance shoots for publications and parks, and uses his slides in lectures.

He has spoken at a wide range of venues, among them the American Museum of Natural History, the Buffalo Museum of Science, the Adirondack Museum, the Adirondack Ecological Center, the Adirondack Park Agency's Visitor Interpretive Centers, the Cornell University Laboratory of Ornithology, the New York Botanical Garden, the State Universities of Albany and Oneonta, Paul Smith's College, the Mohonk Mountain House, the Westchester chapter of the American College of Surgeons, and professional conferences, garden clubs, and Audubon societies in many states.

Ed has two new books in progress: a novel about Henry Hudson and a narrative of wildlife, homesteading, and home renovation in the Adirondack Mountains.

Ed, his wife, Debbie, and children Ned and Tasman live on the Saranac River in New York's six million acre Adirondack Park.